The story of a man who spent his whole life alone

As I grew older I realised I had lived a paralell life to Van Gogh. A life time alone in desolate places.Eventually I came to the conclusion that I was born after an apocalypse and I tried to capture what I saw in paintings….I wandered the earth for years trying to find anyone who knew the same things as me.Dead cities.Empty airports.Railway stations with two passengers on and eventually I got a house and started painting what I had seen.These are the post apocalyptic places and people I have seen just like van Gogh did.

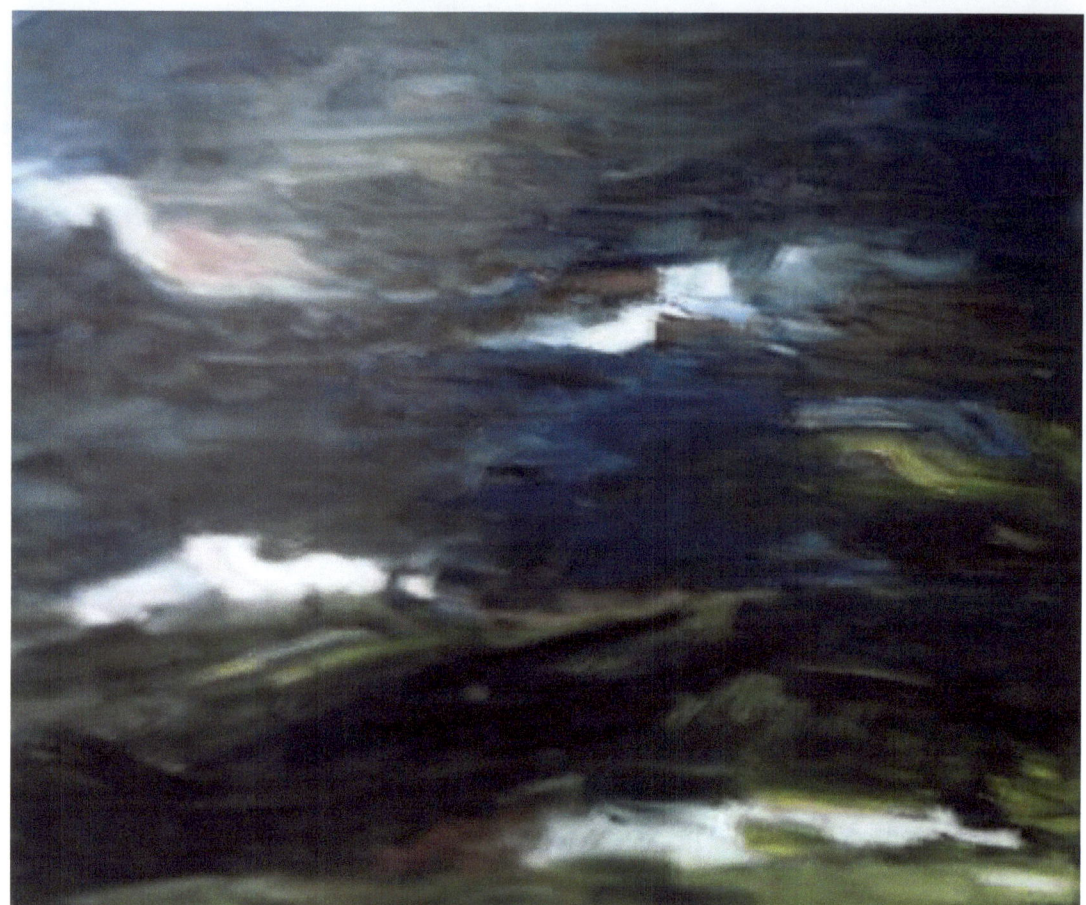

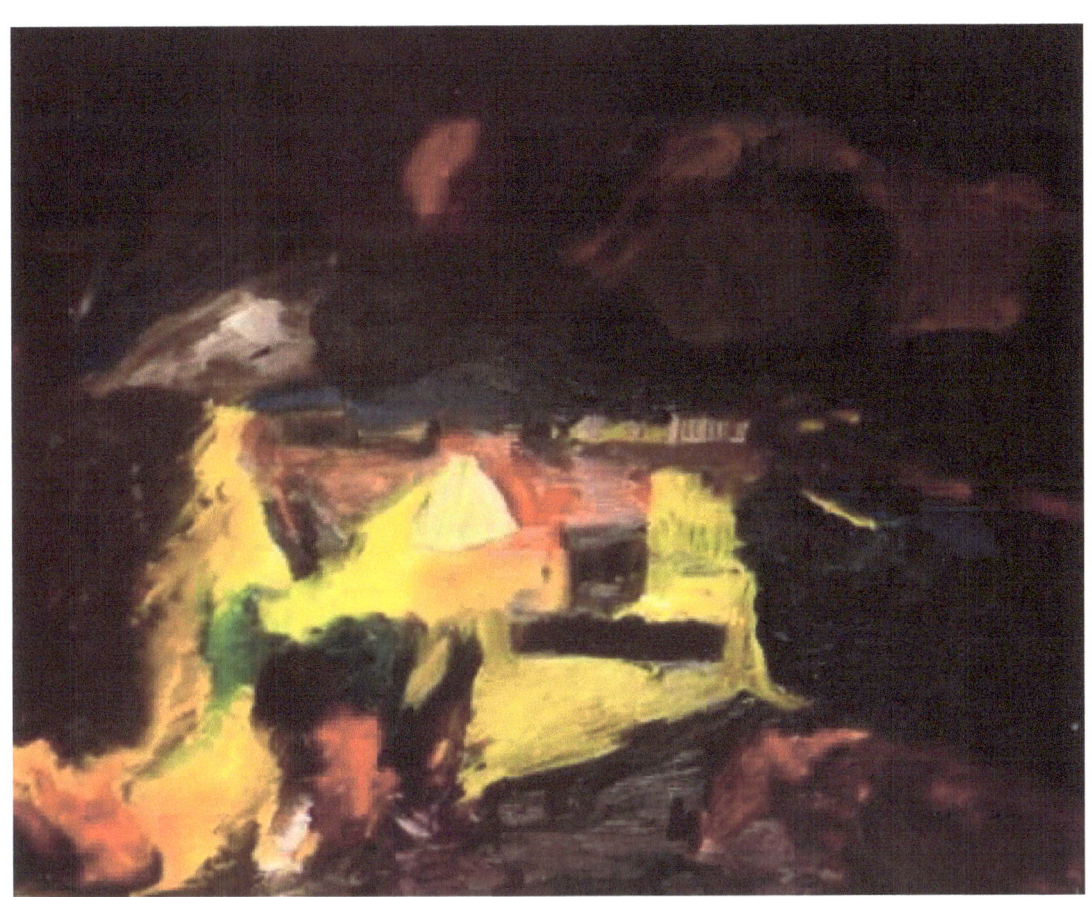

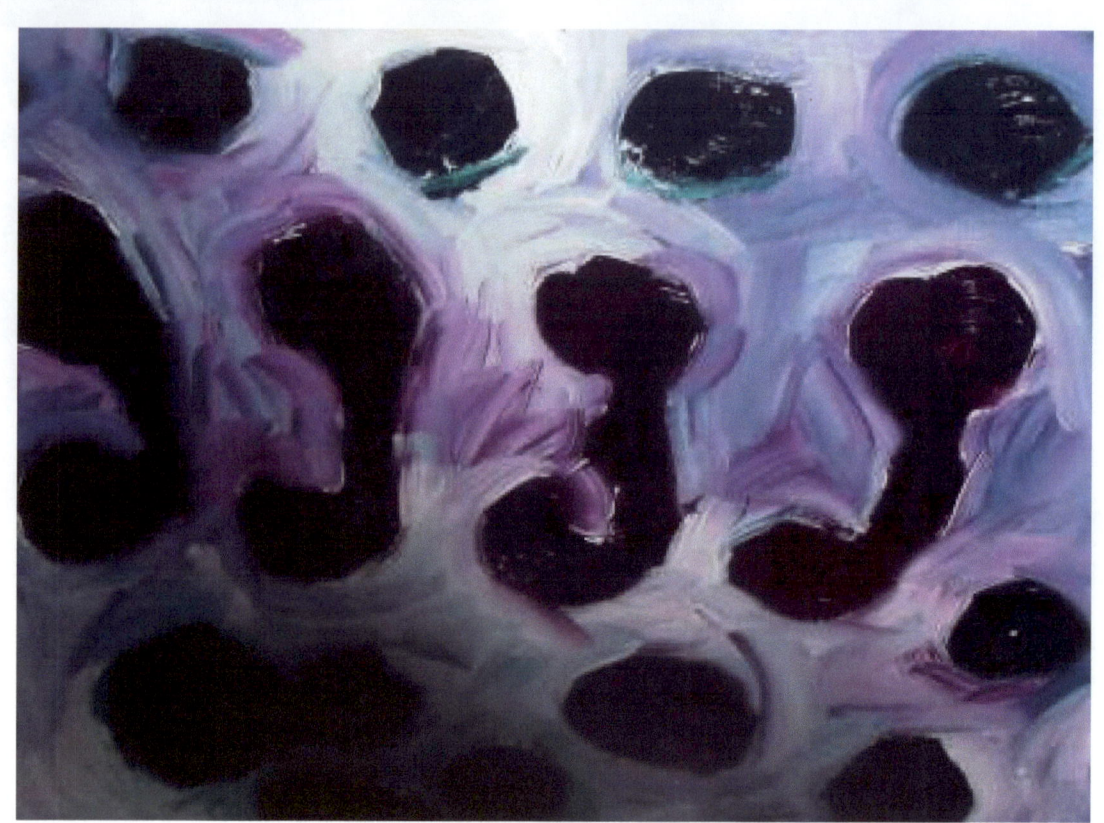

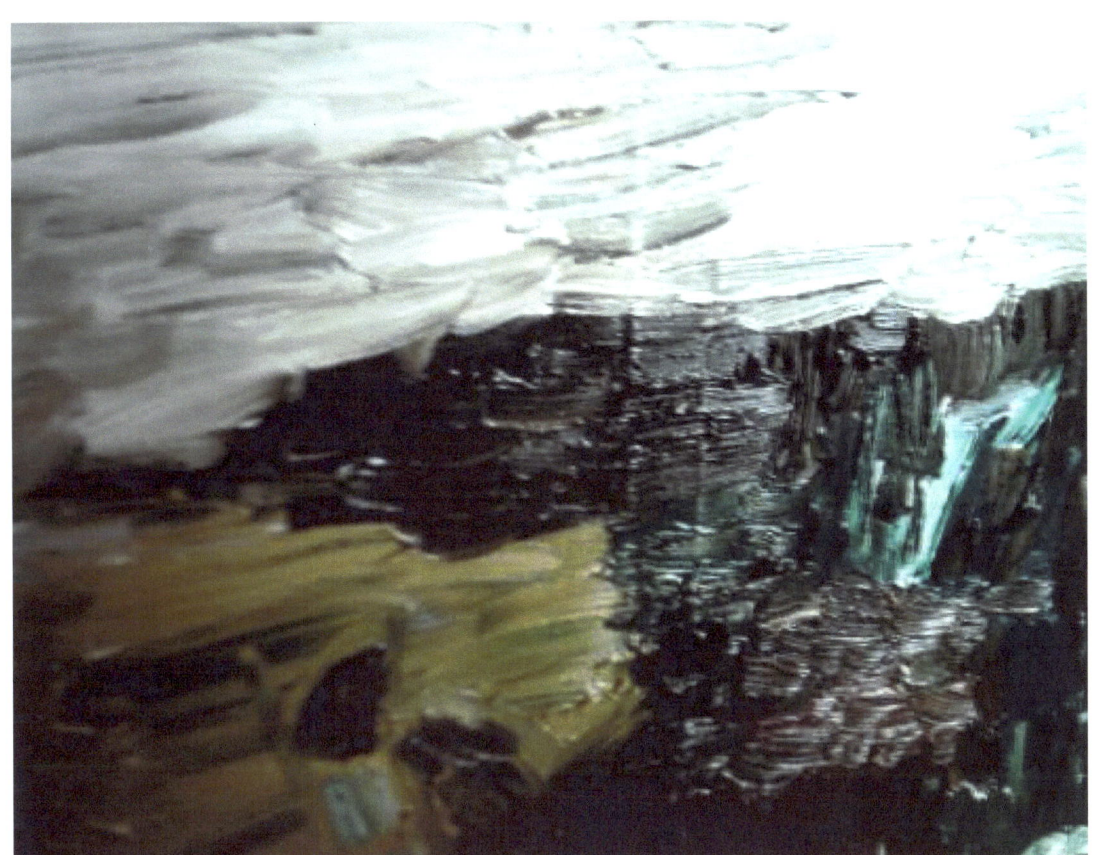

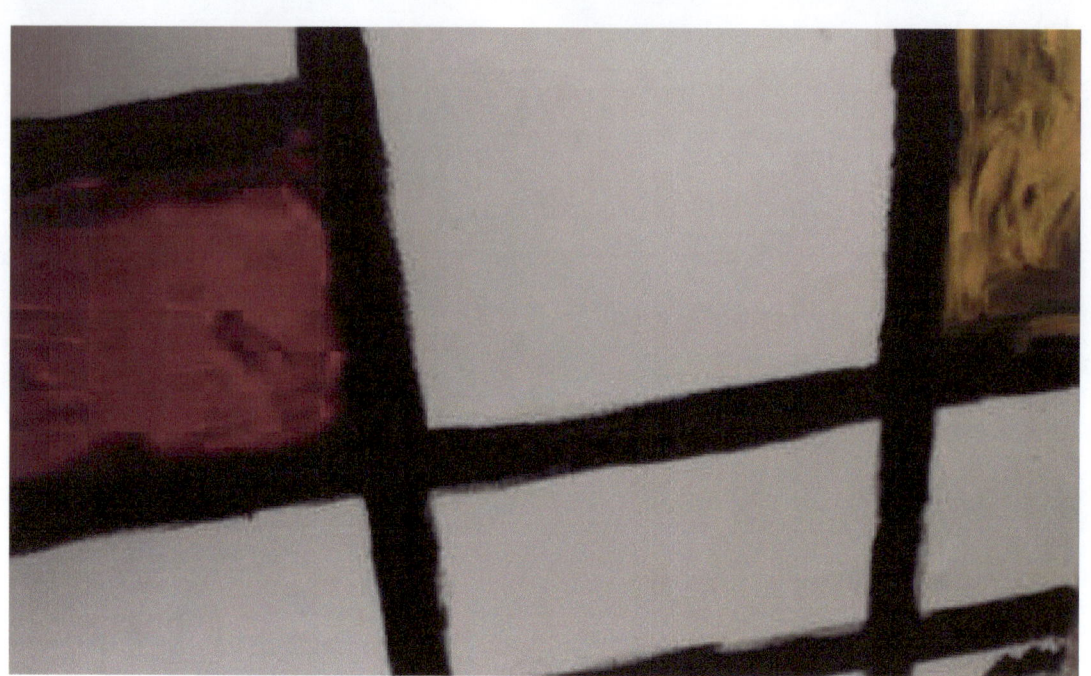

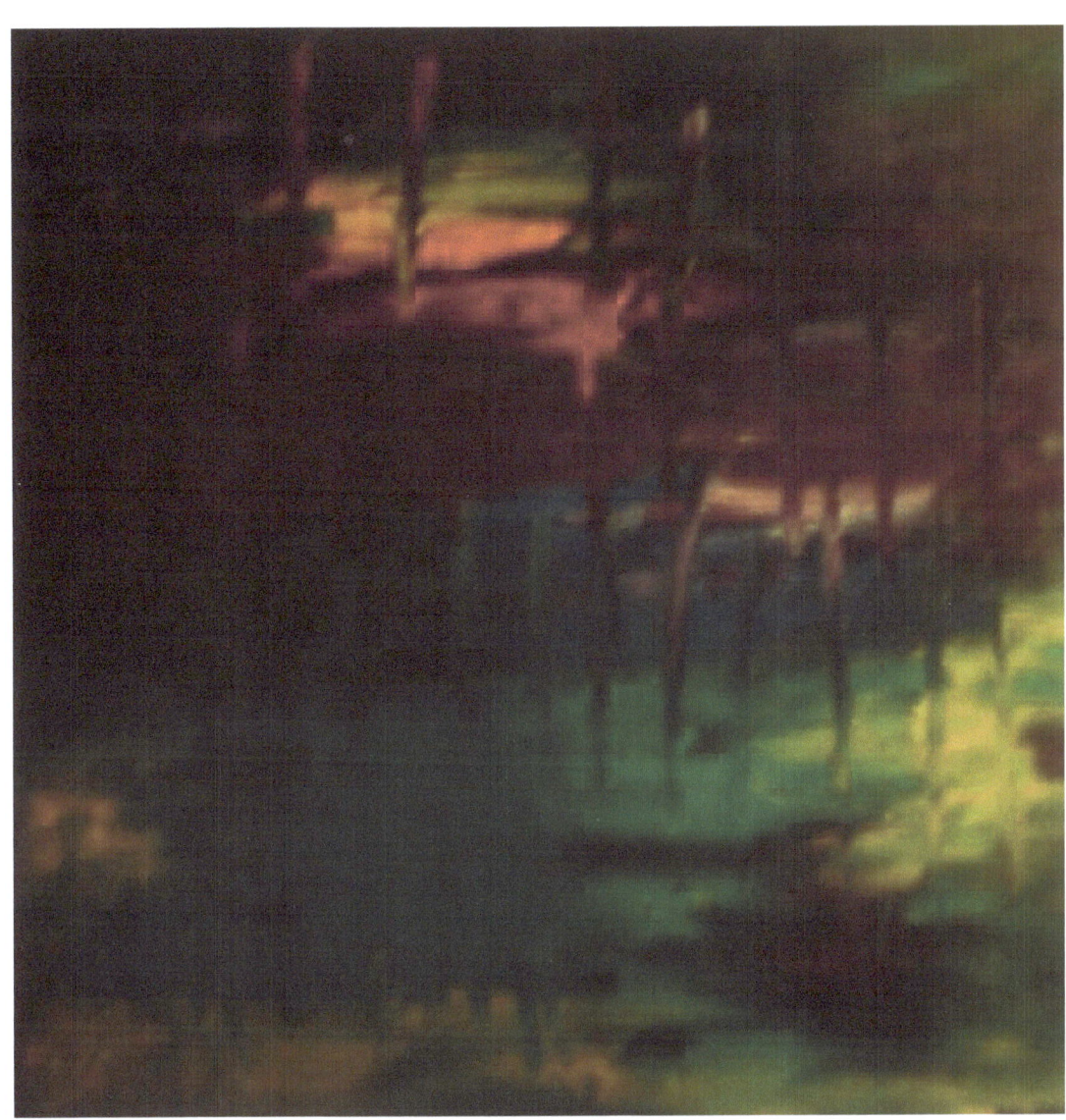

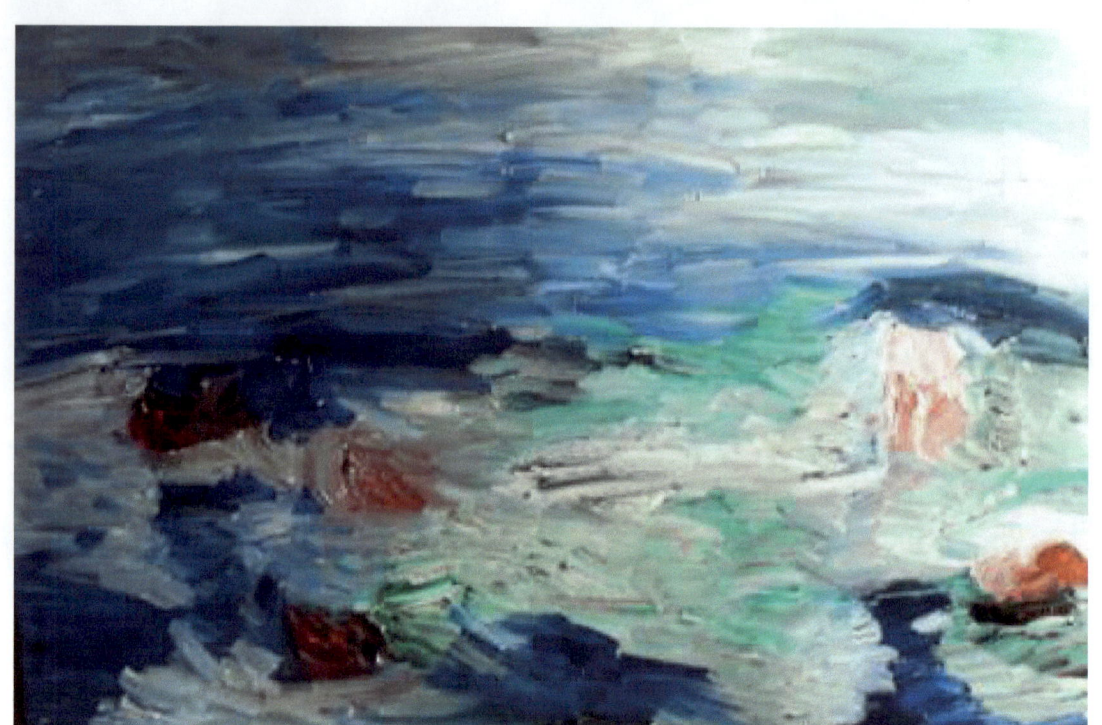

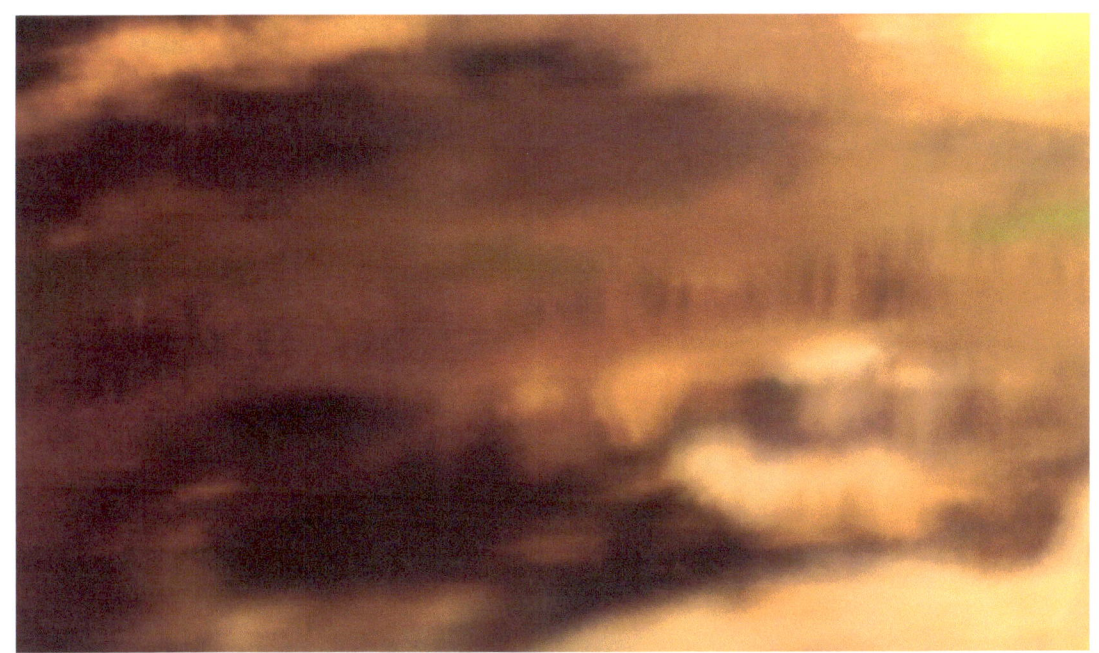

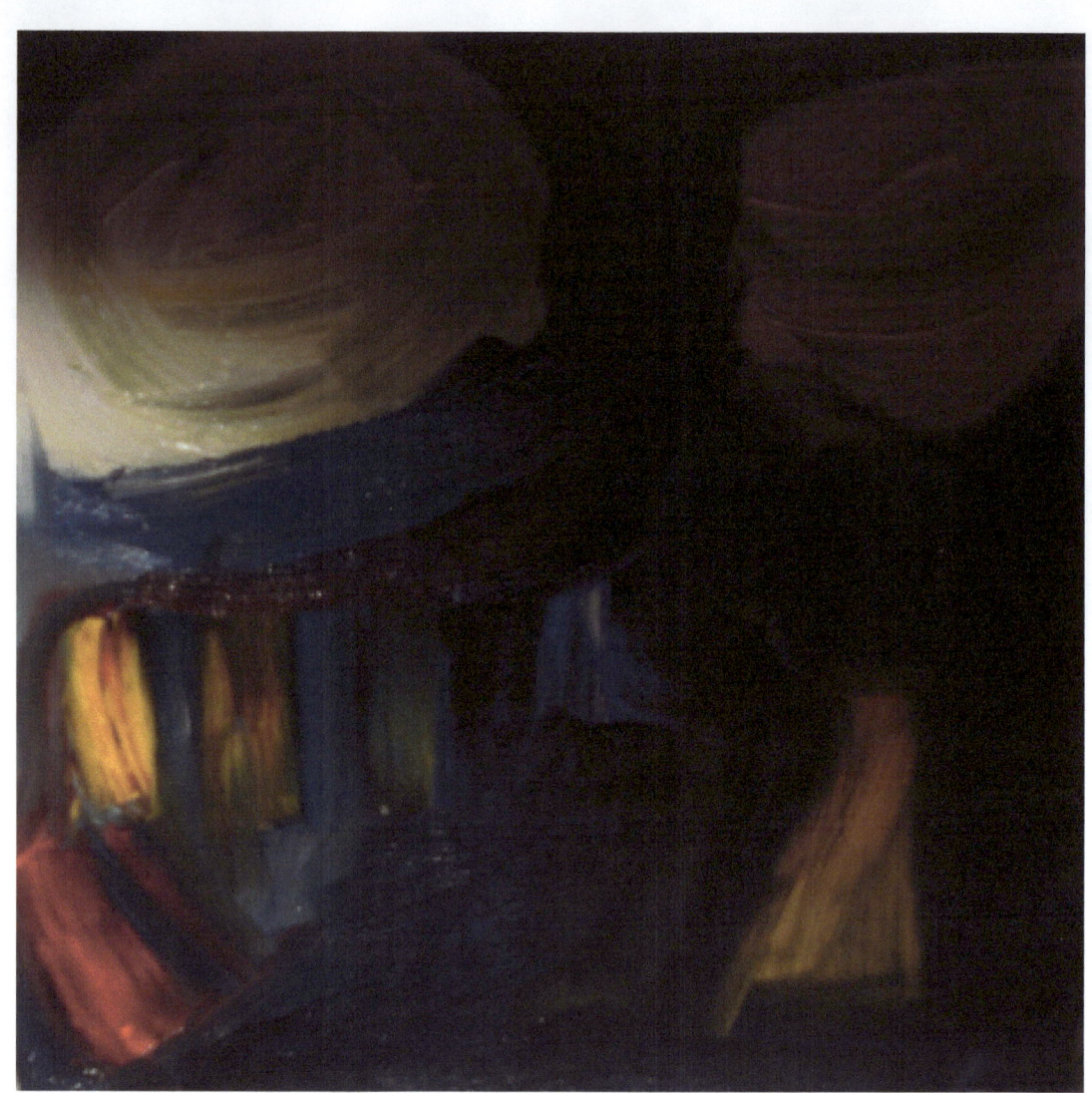

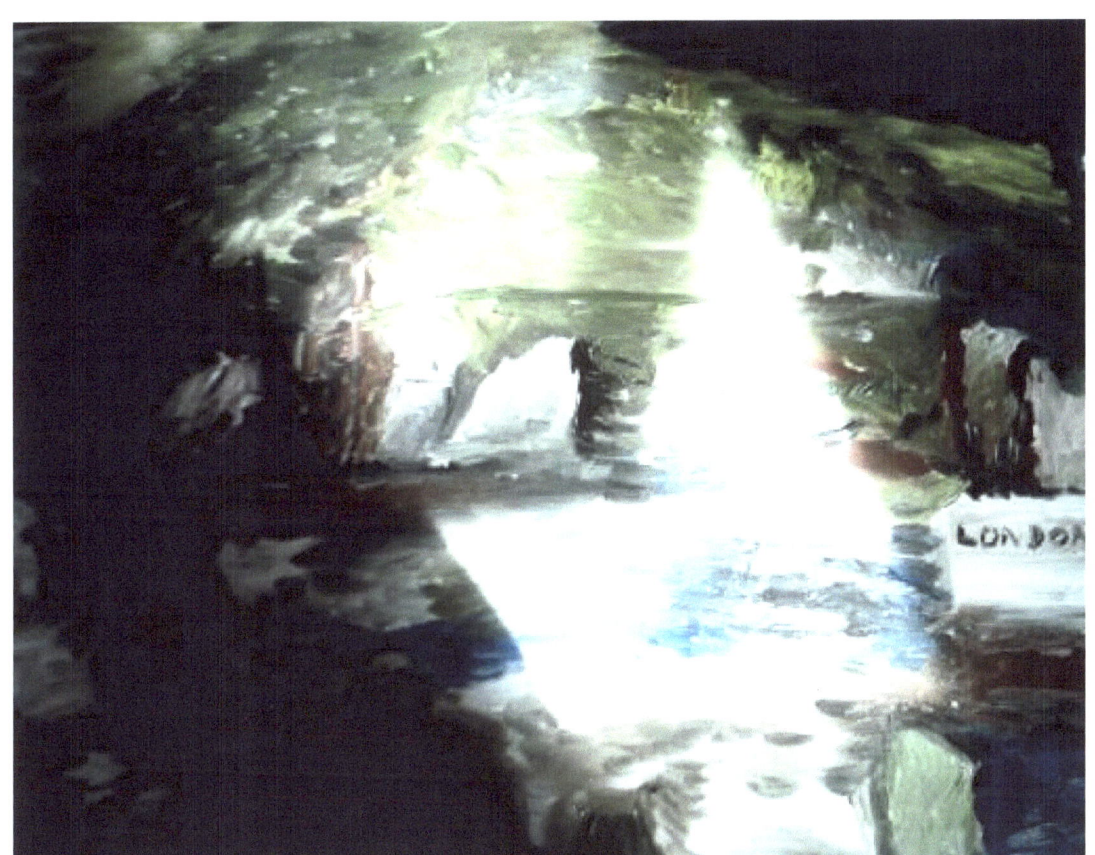

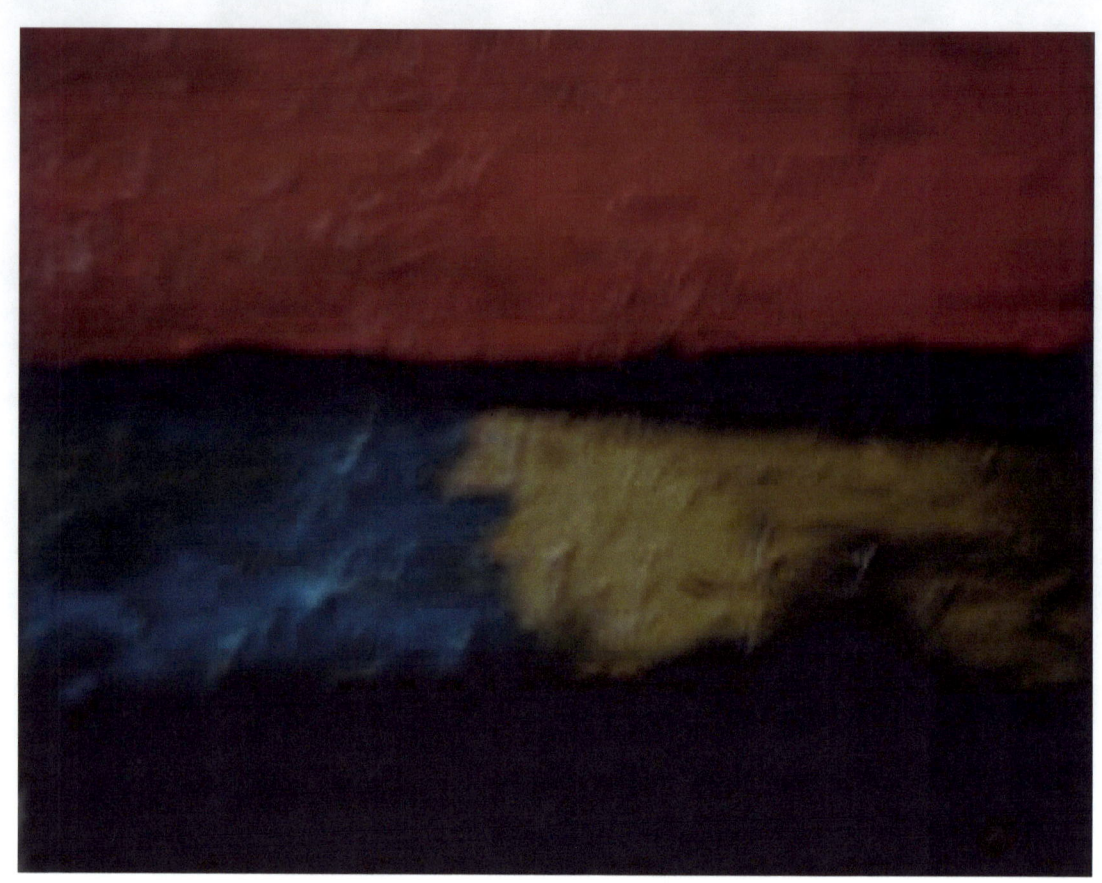

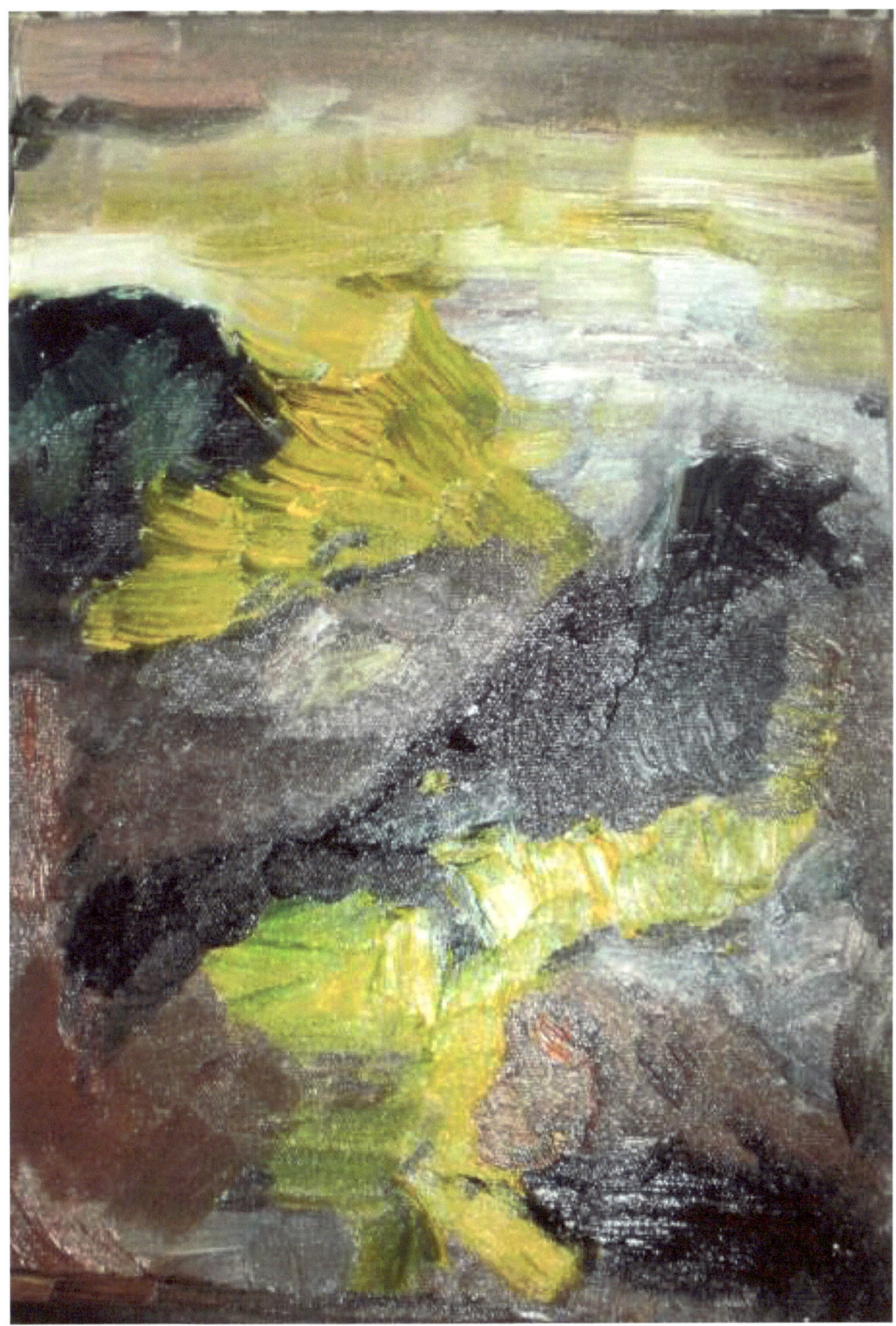

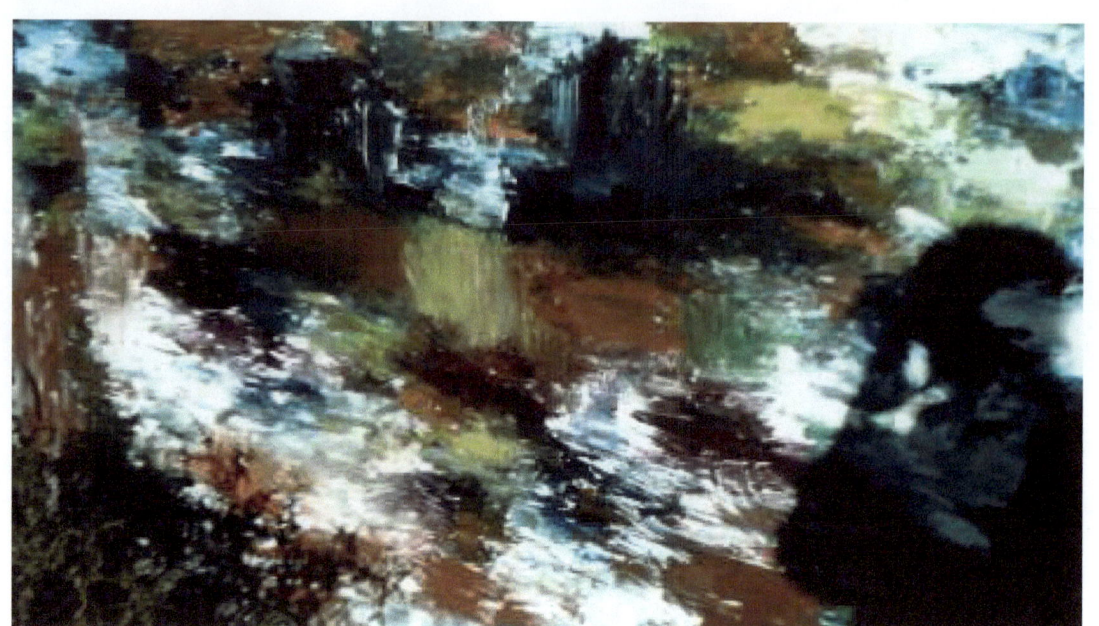

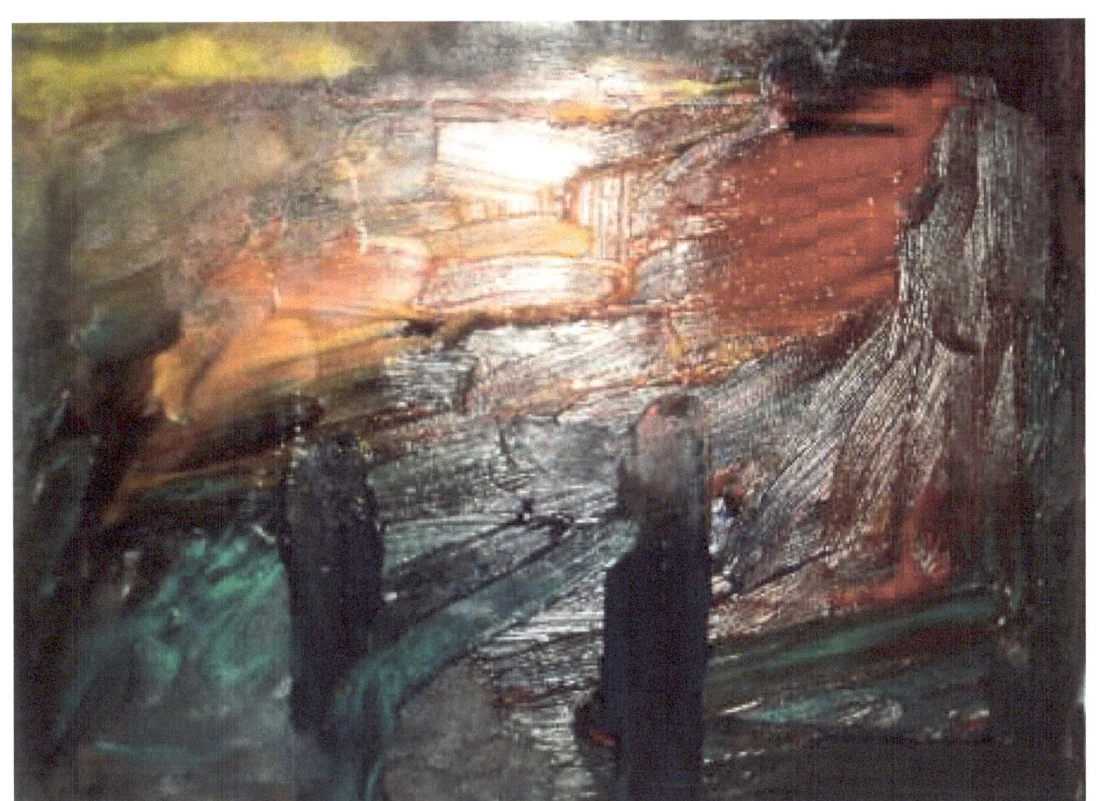

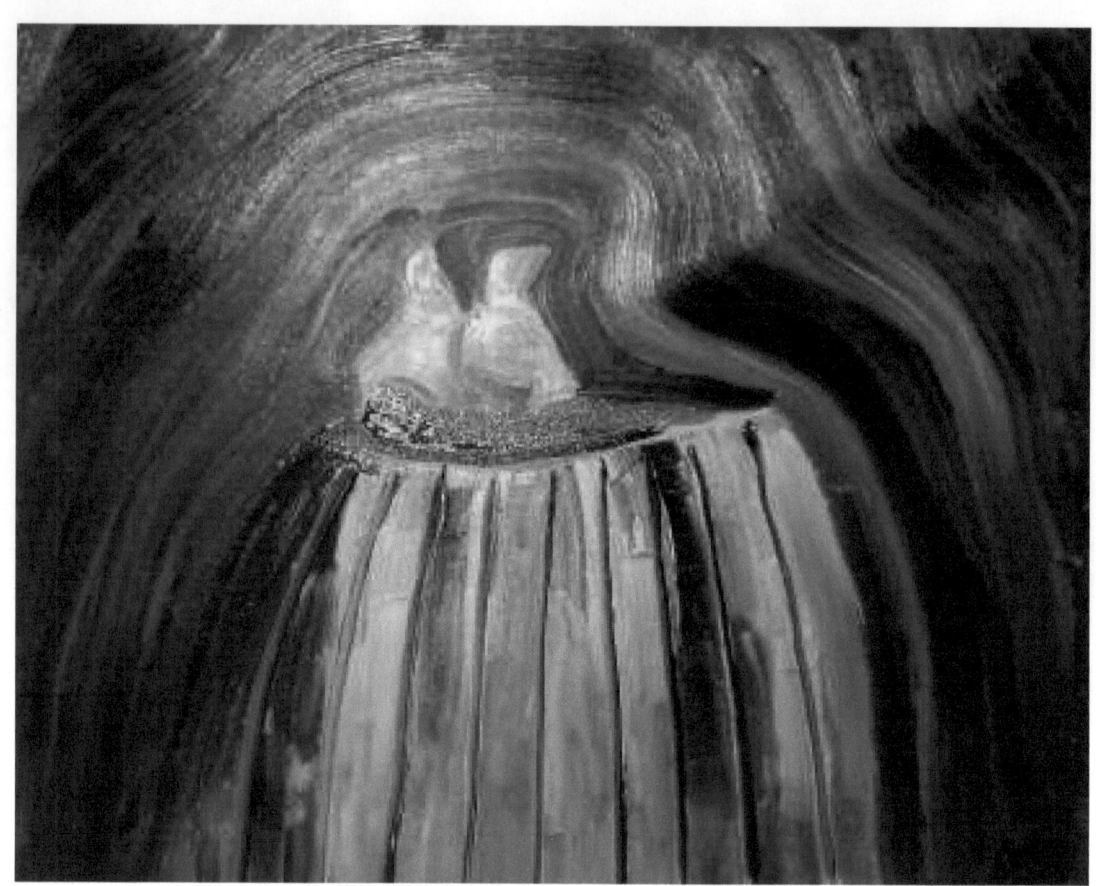

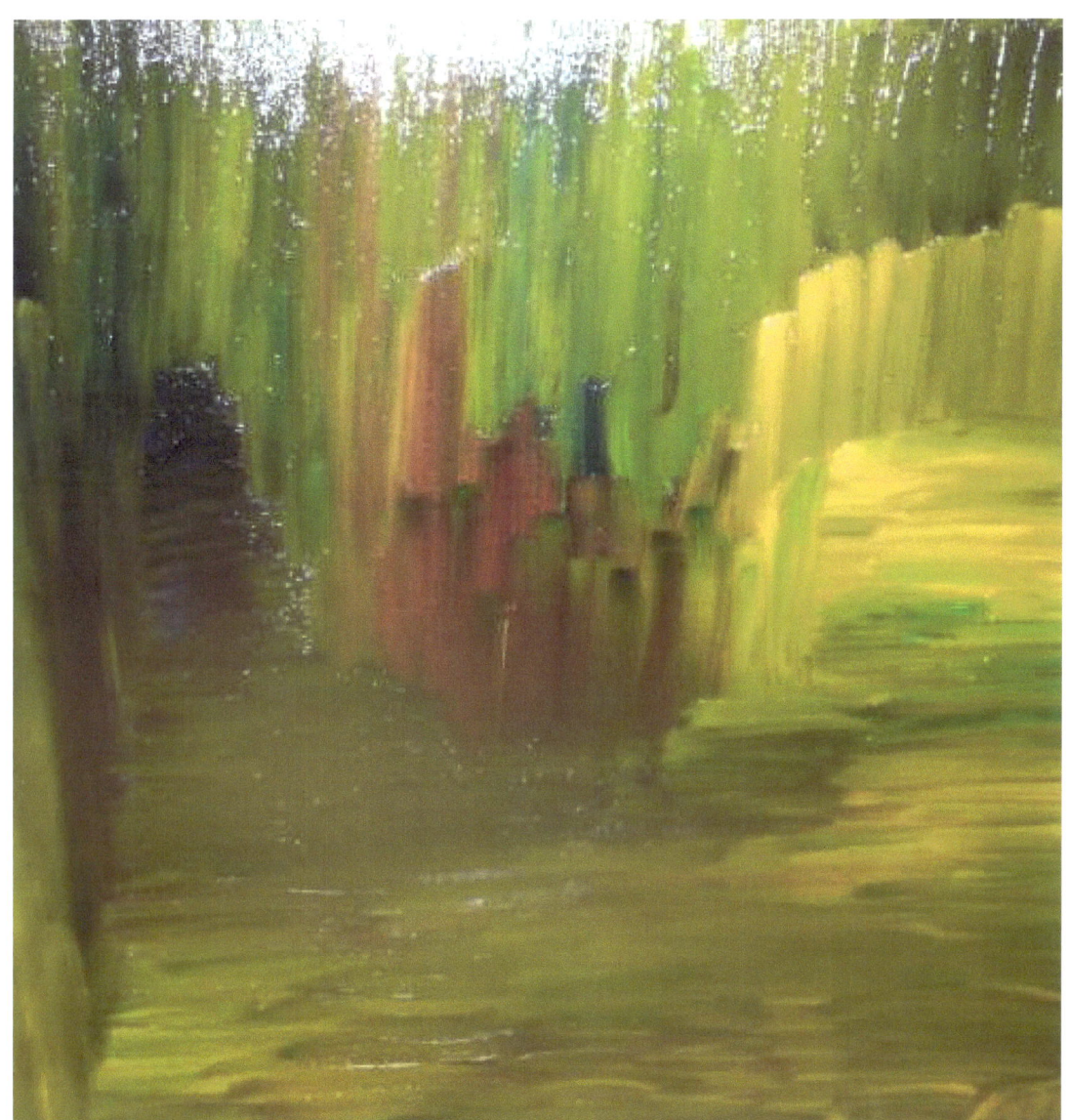

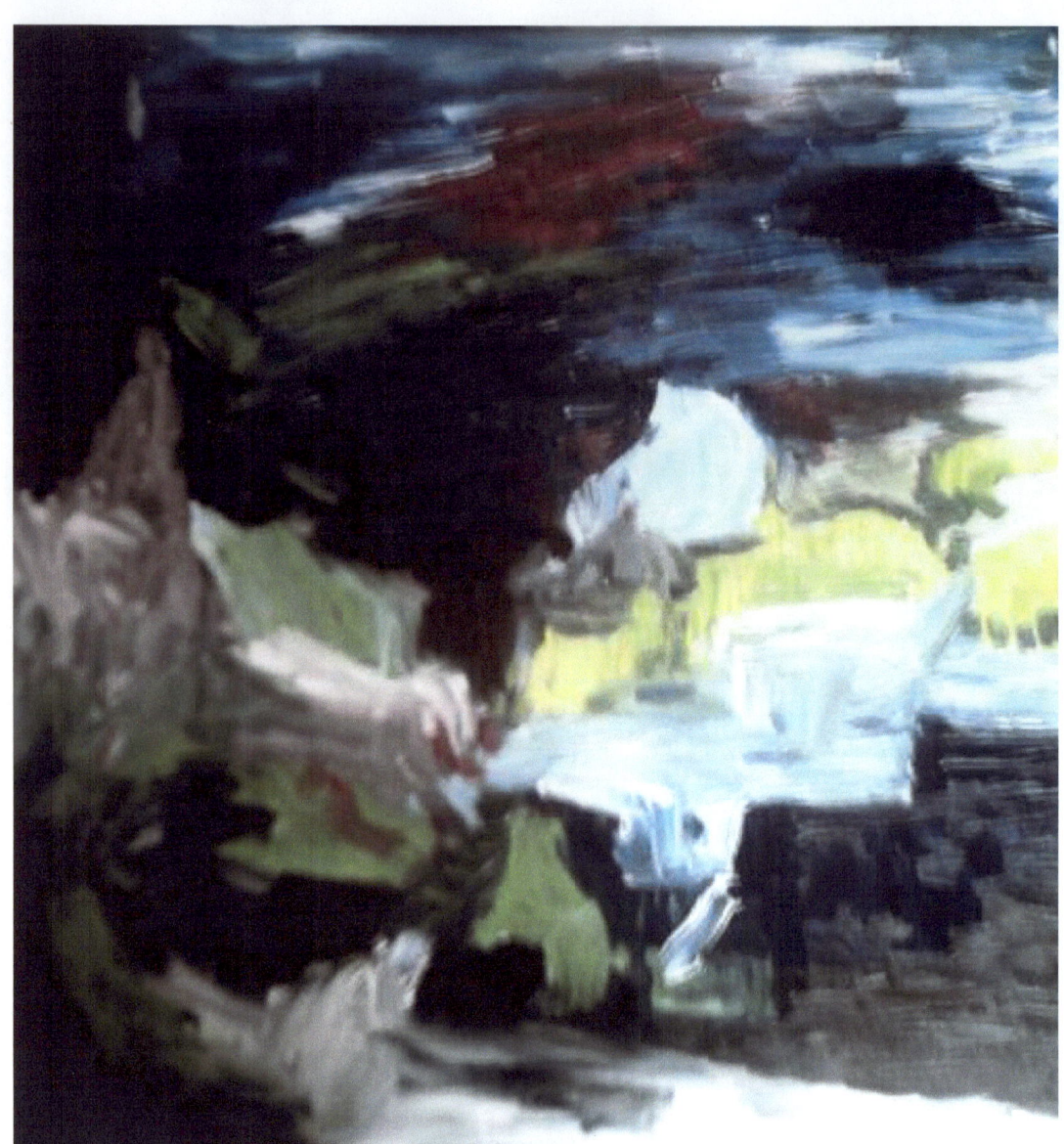

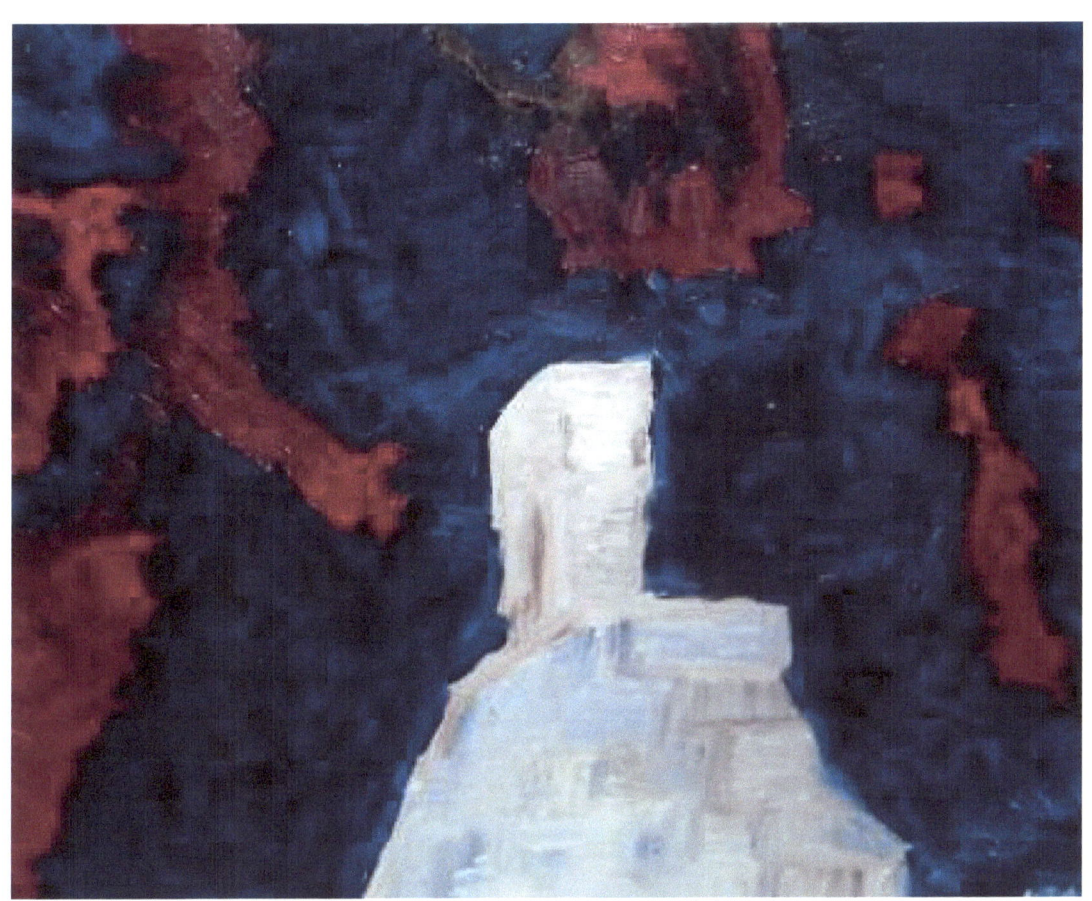

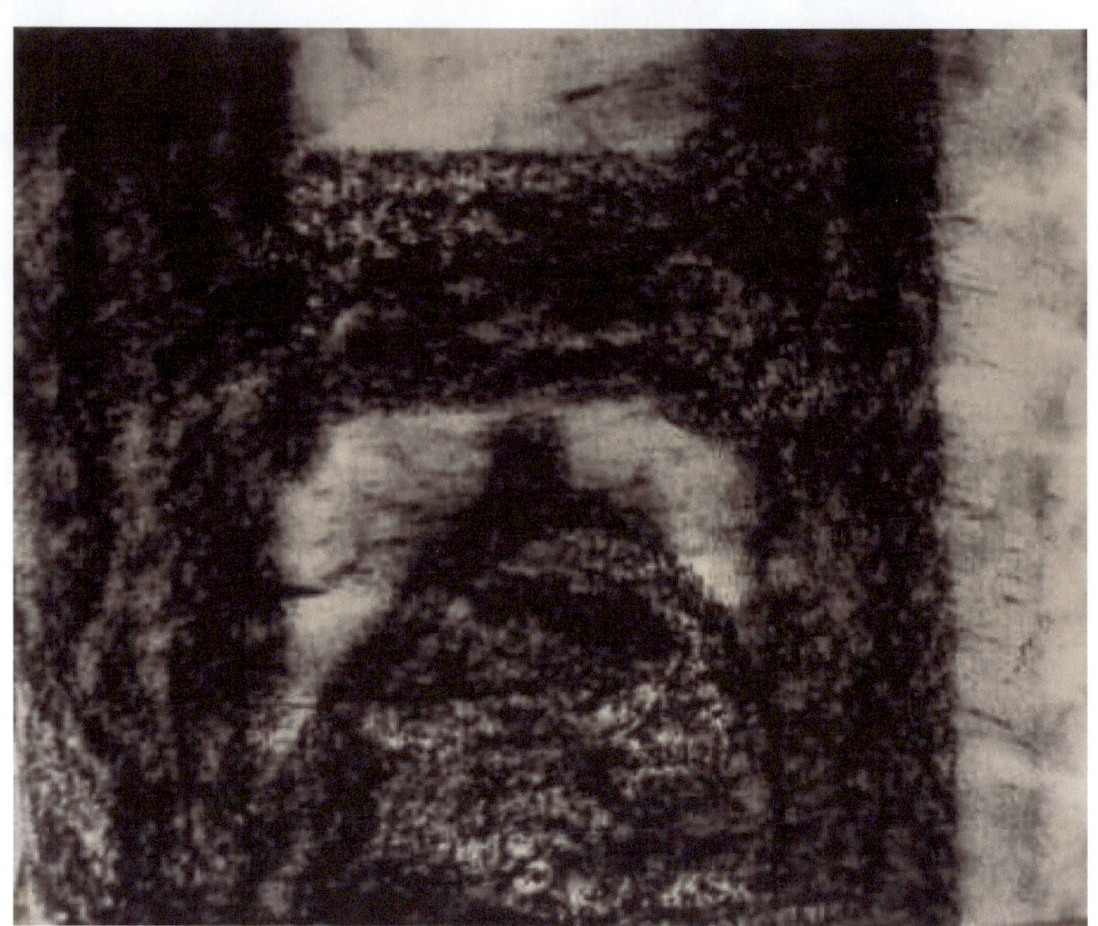

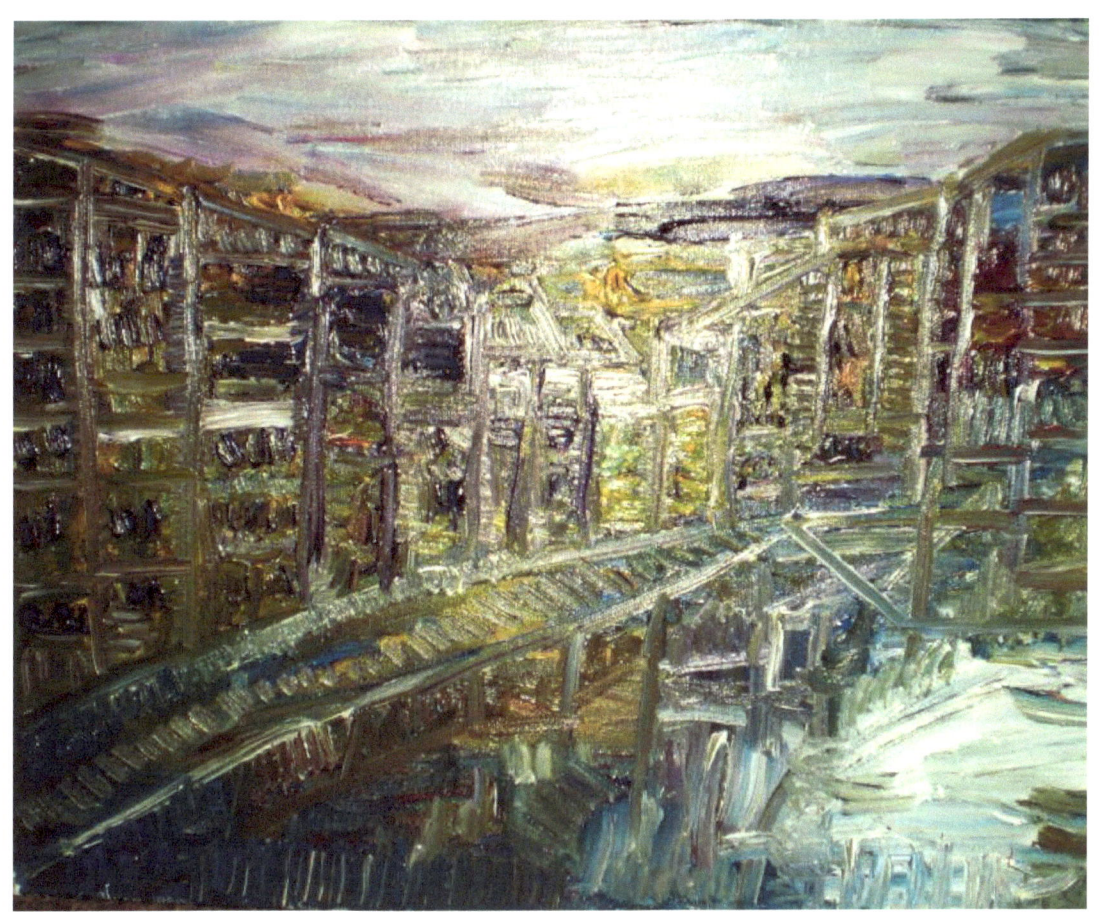

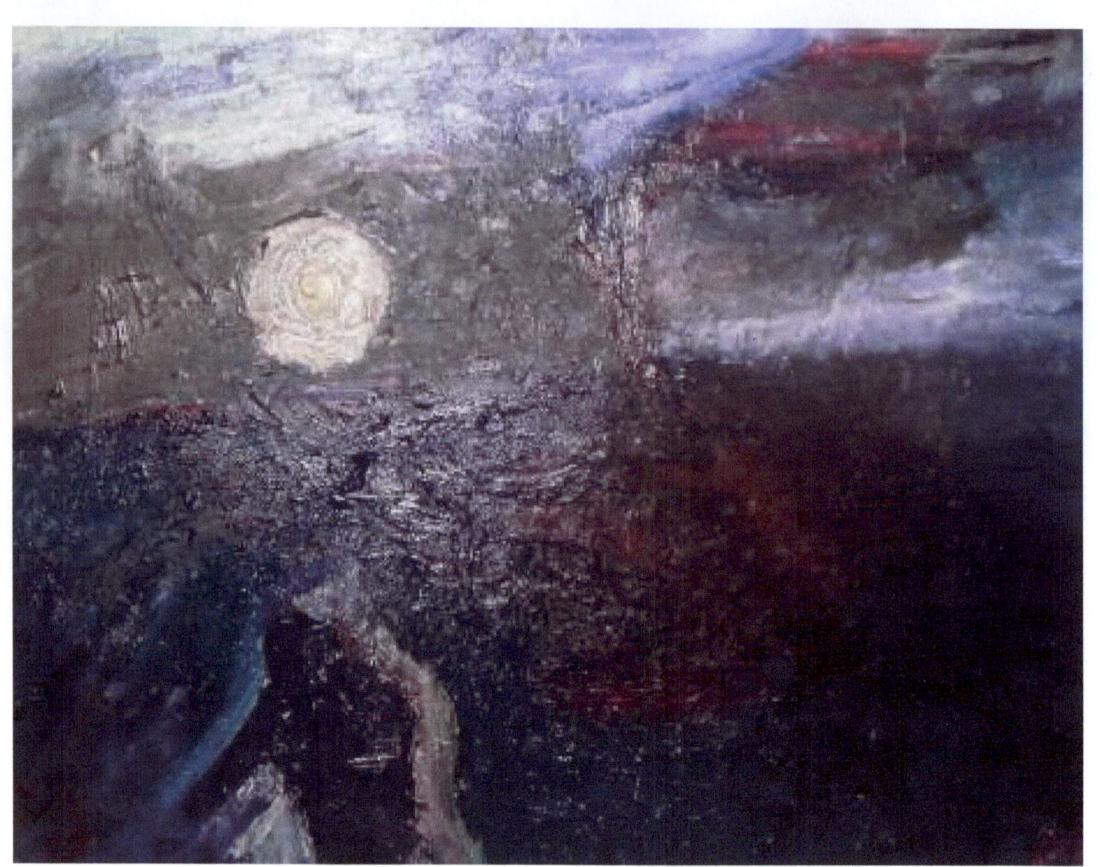

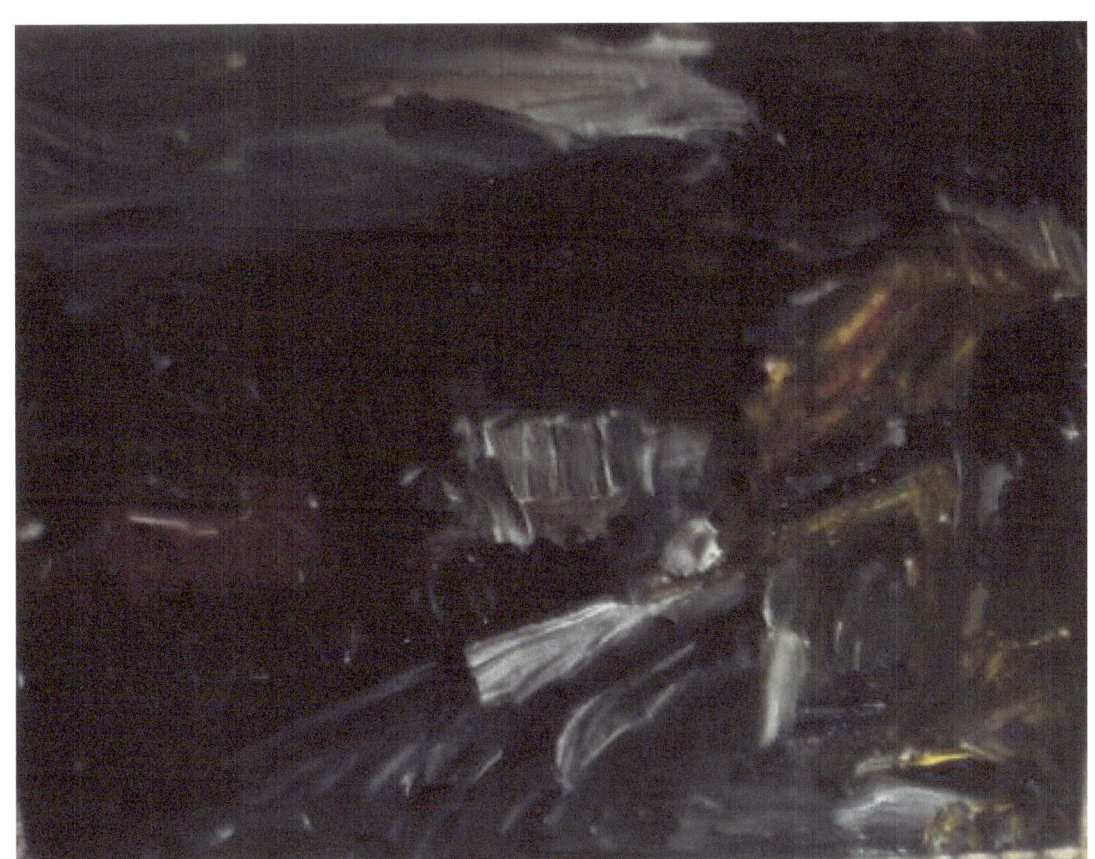

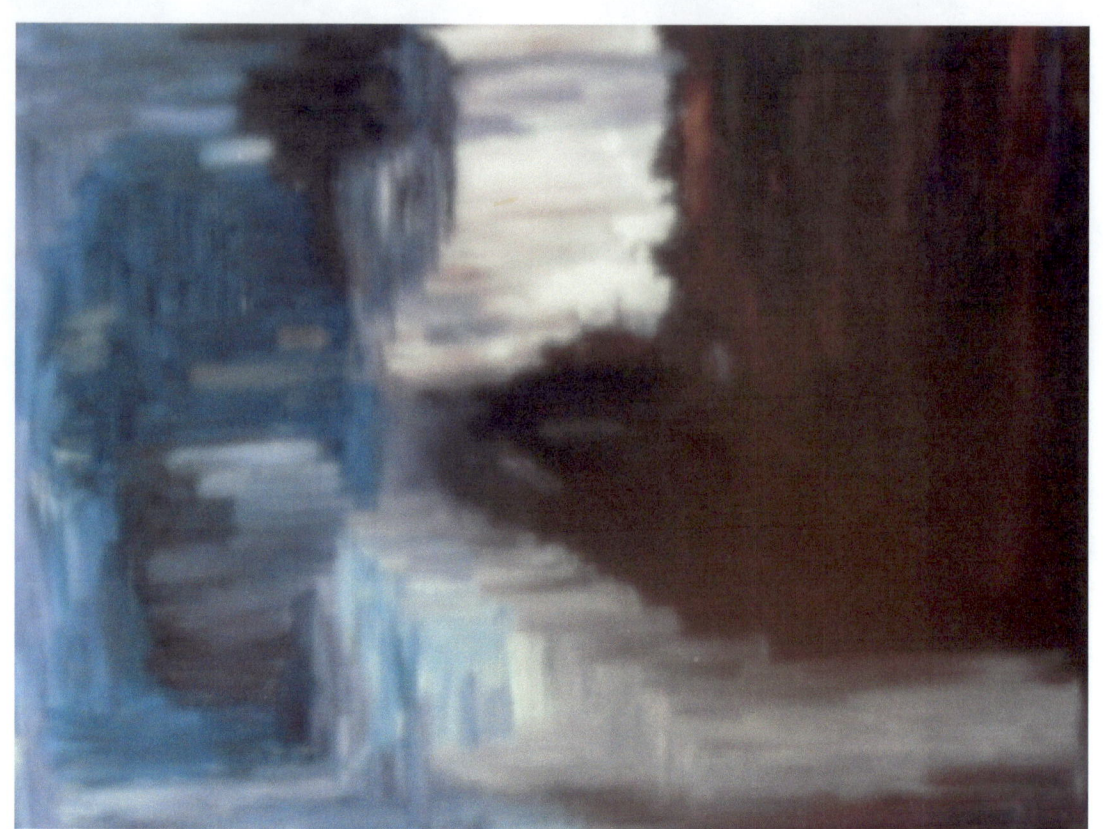

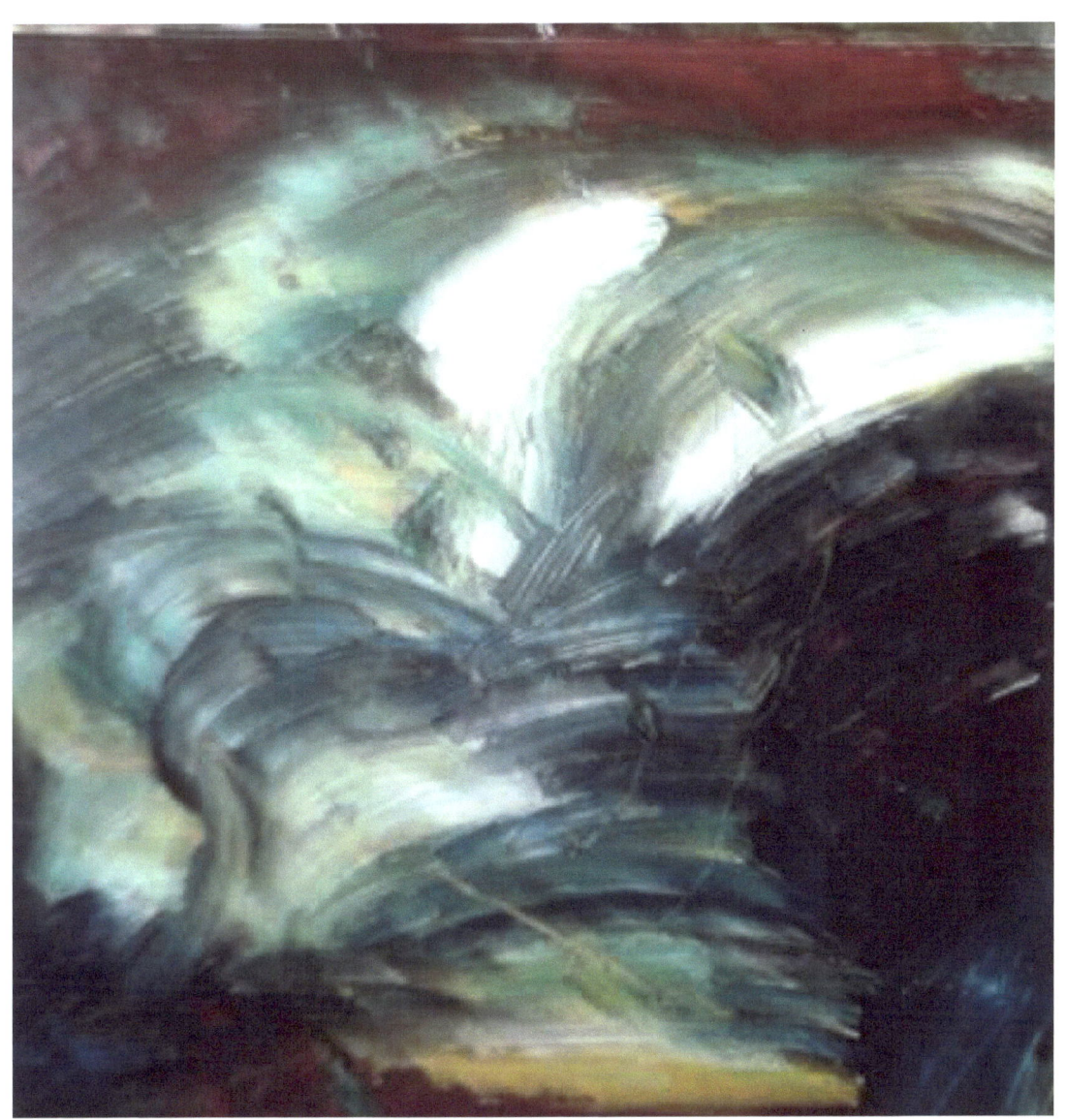

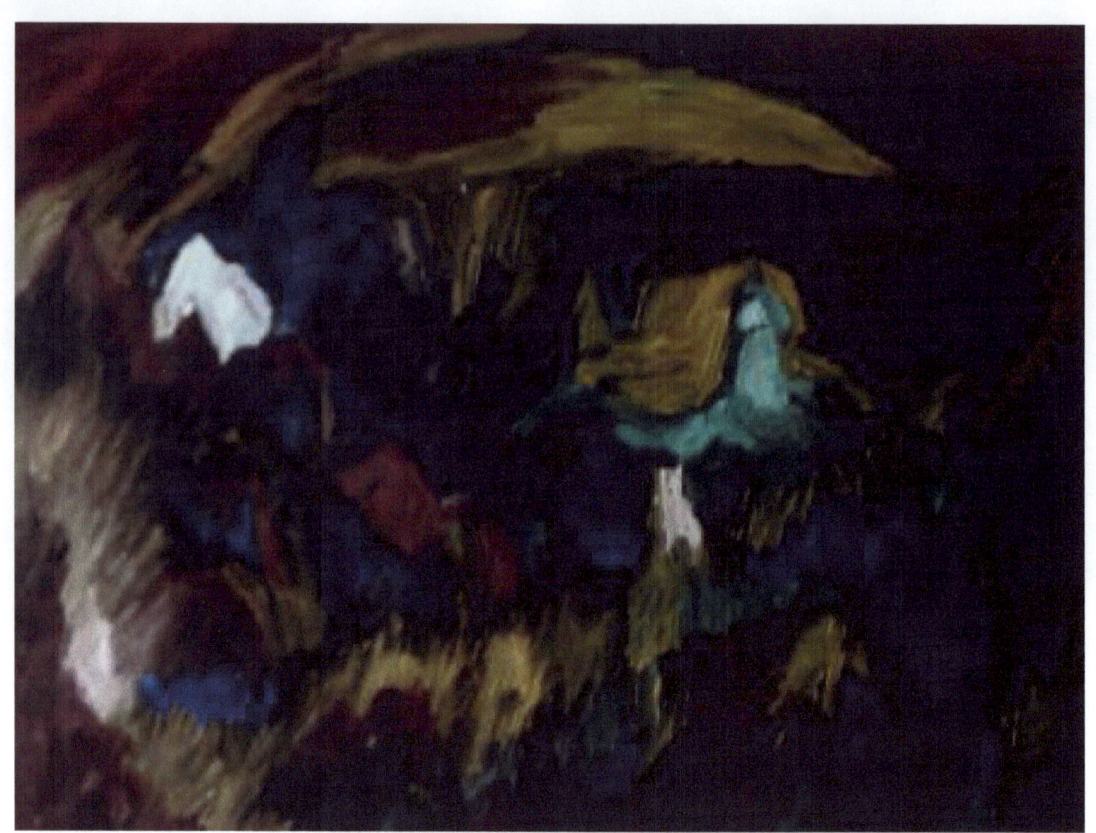

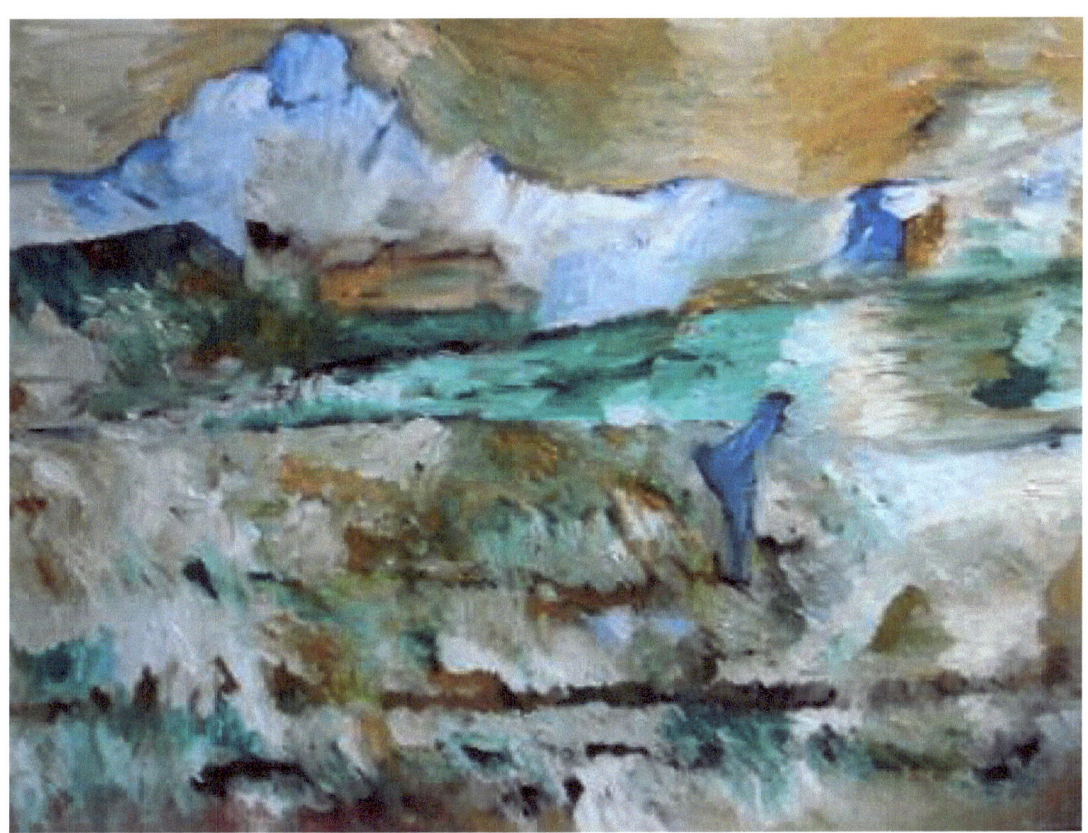

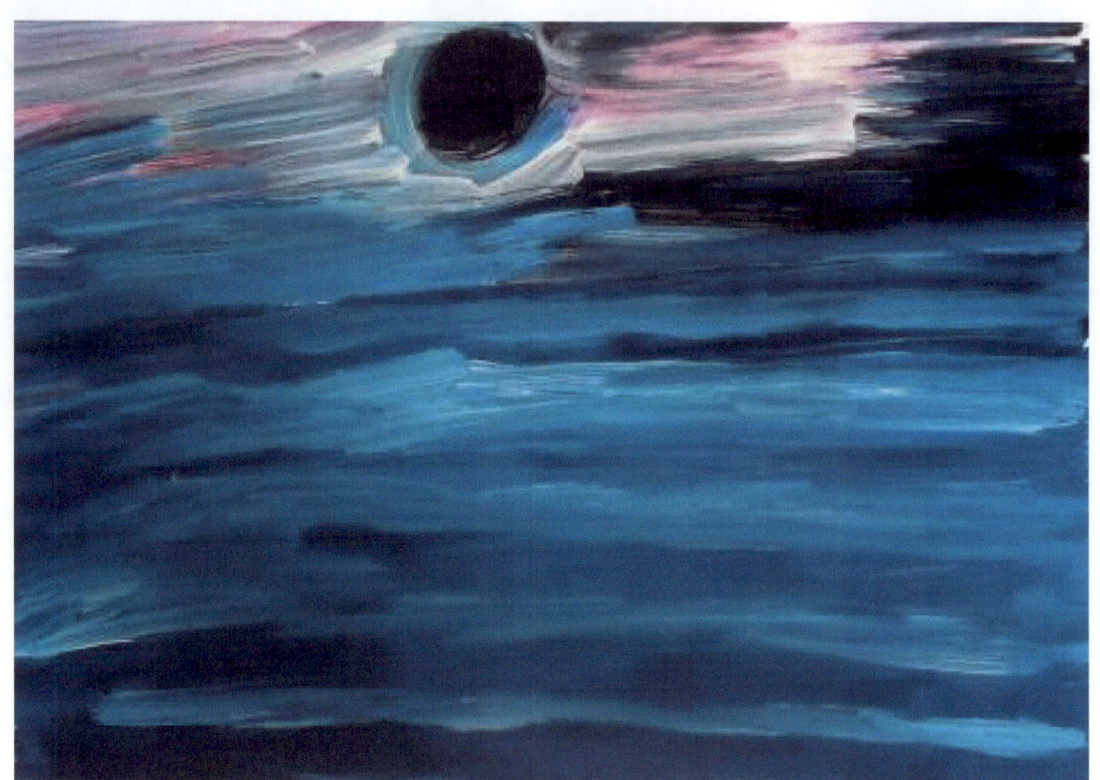

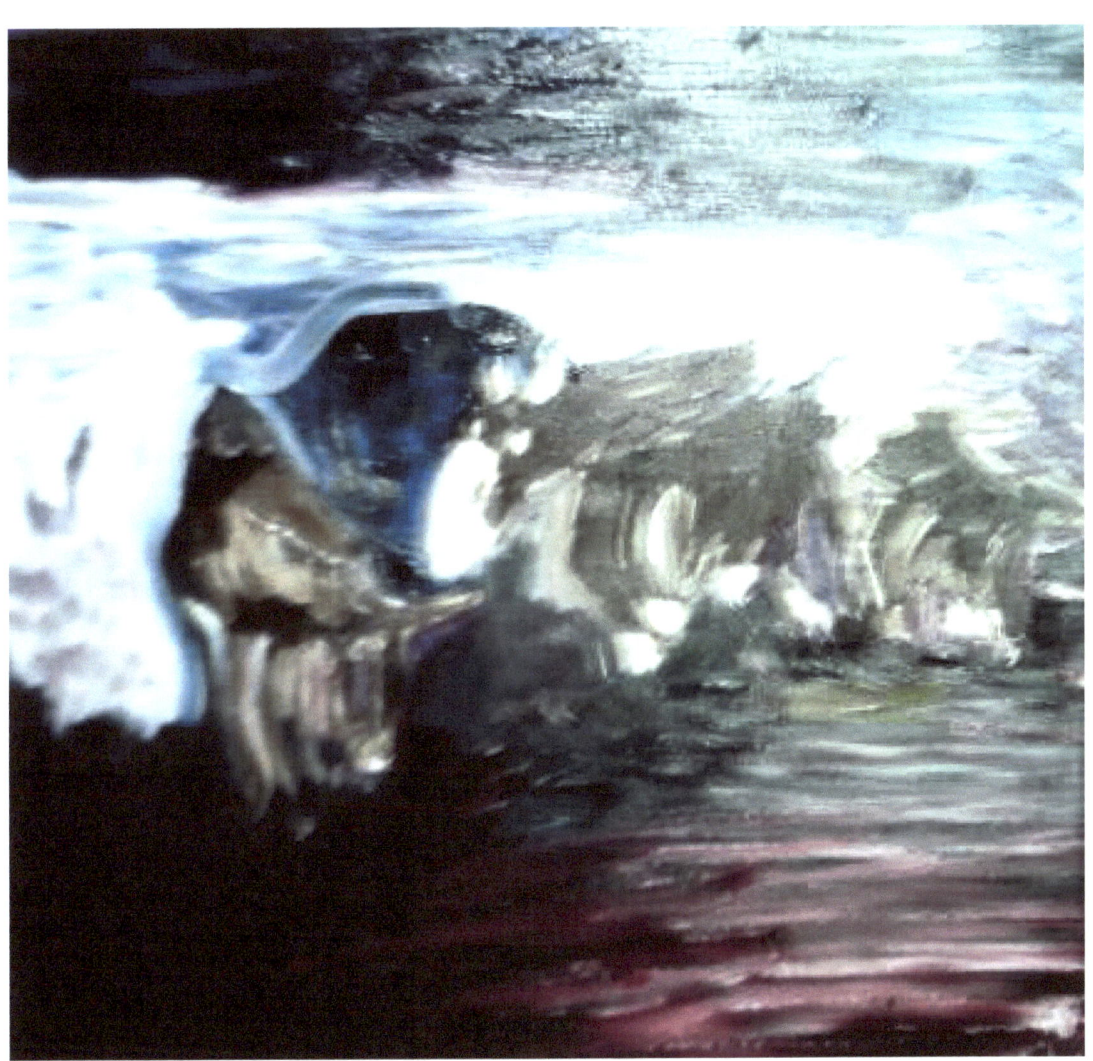

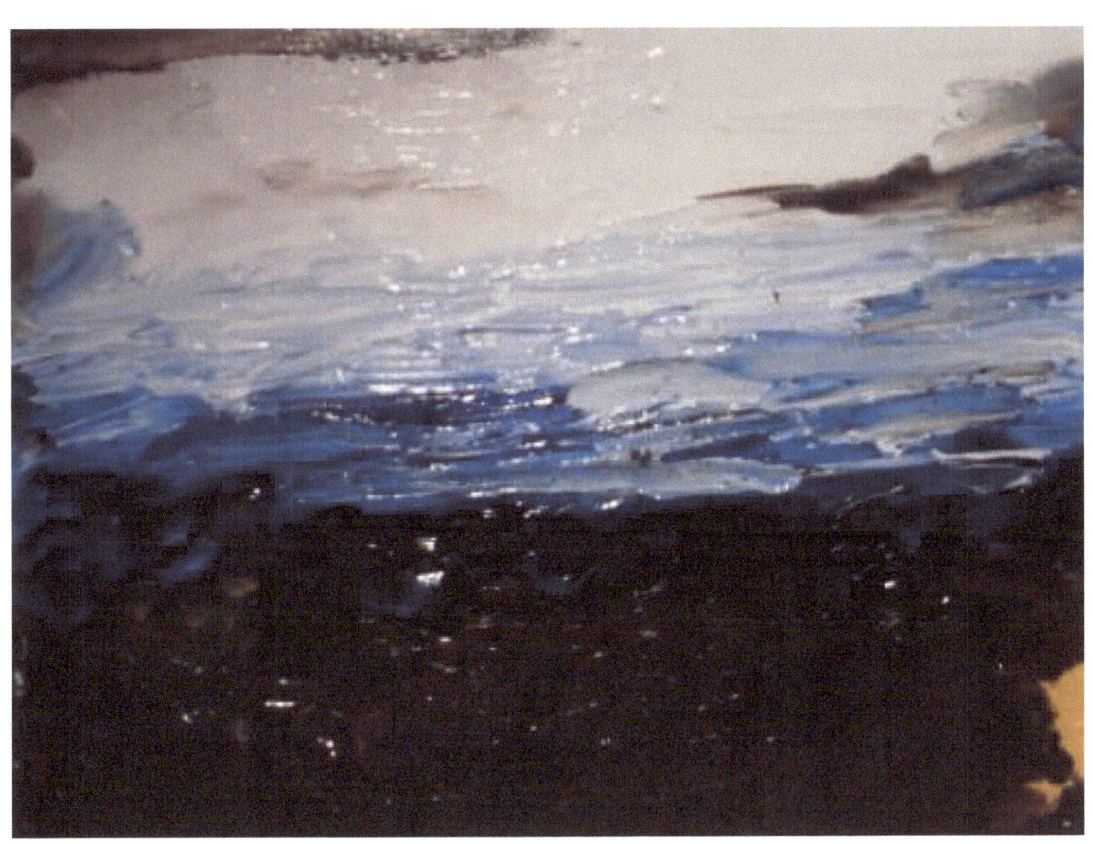

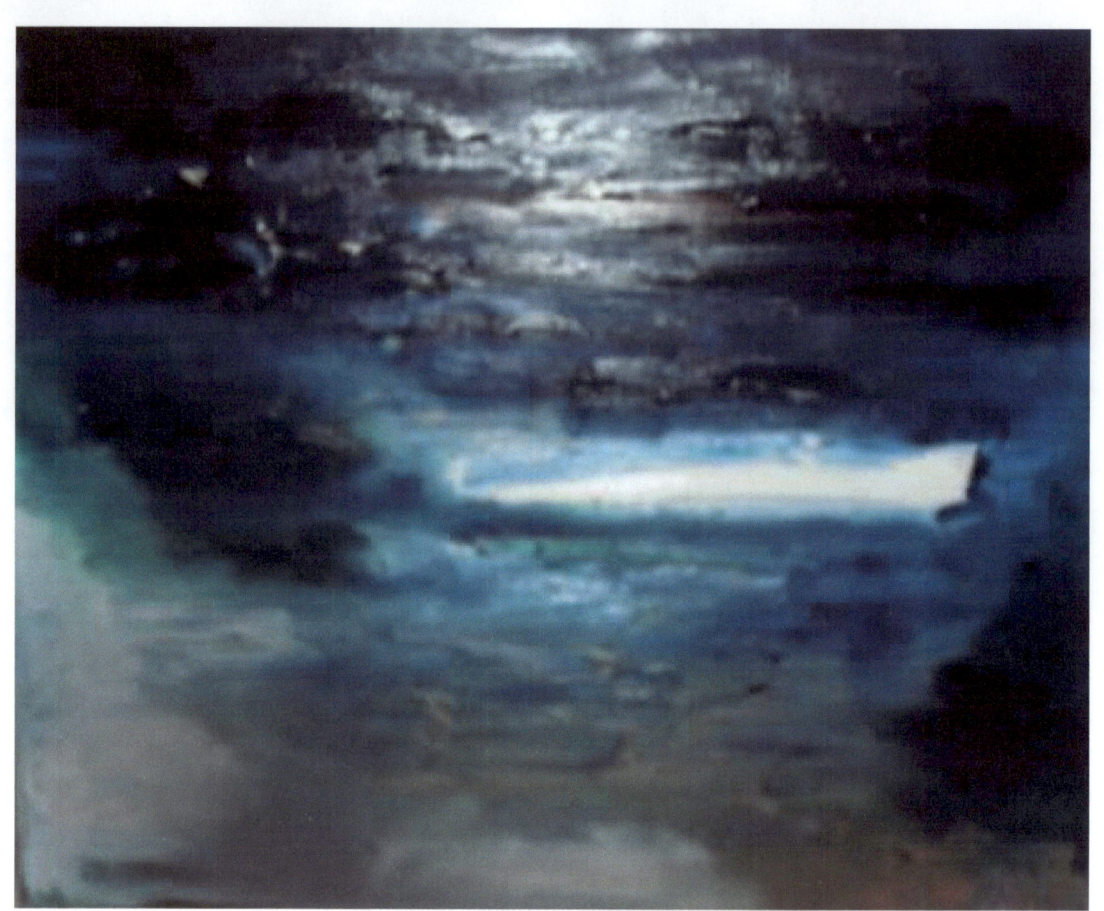

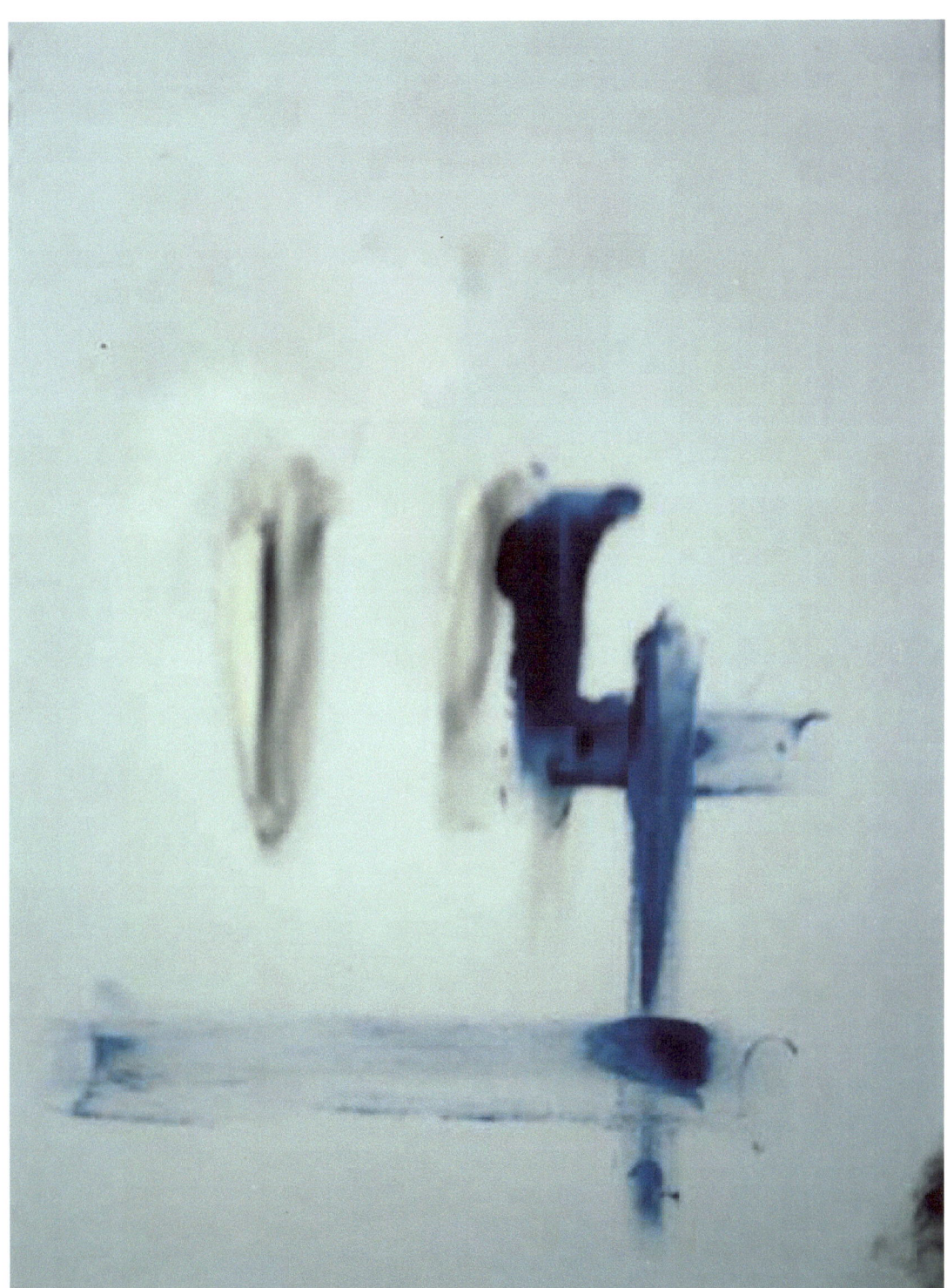

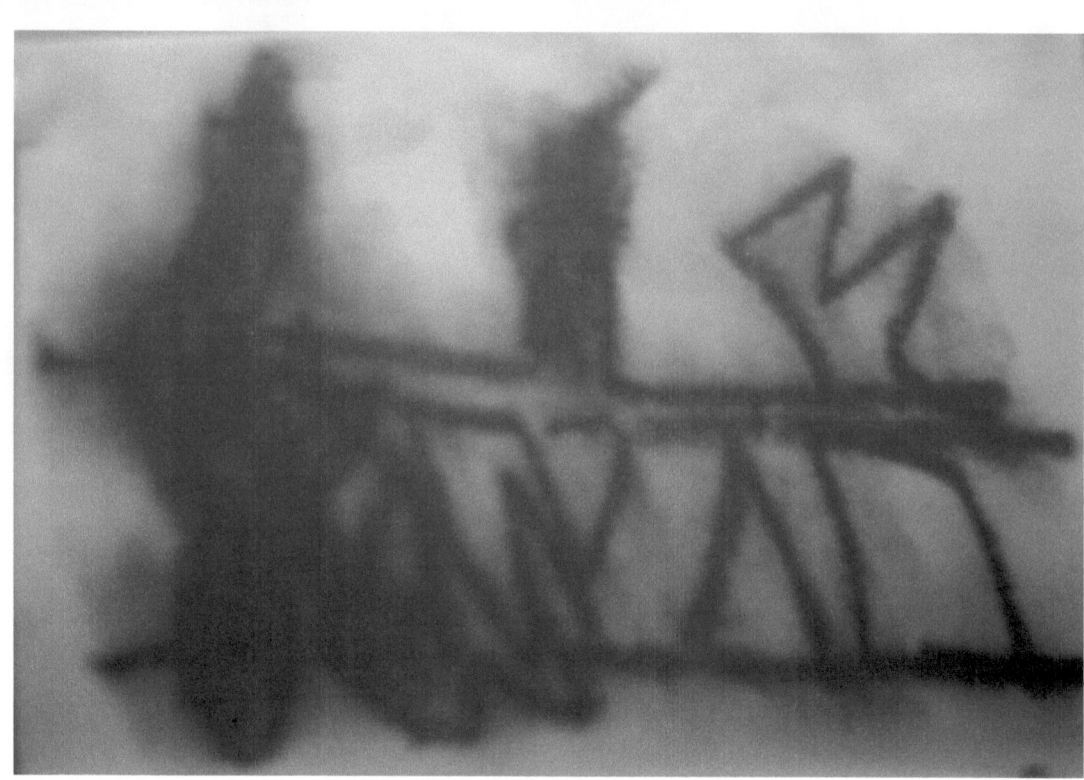

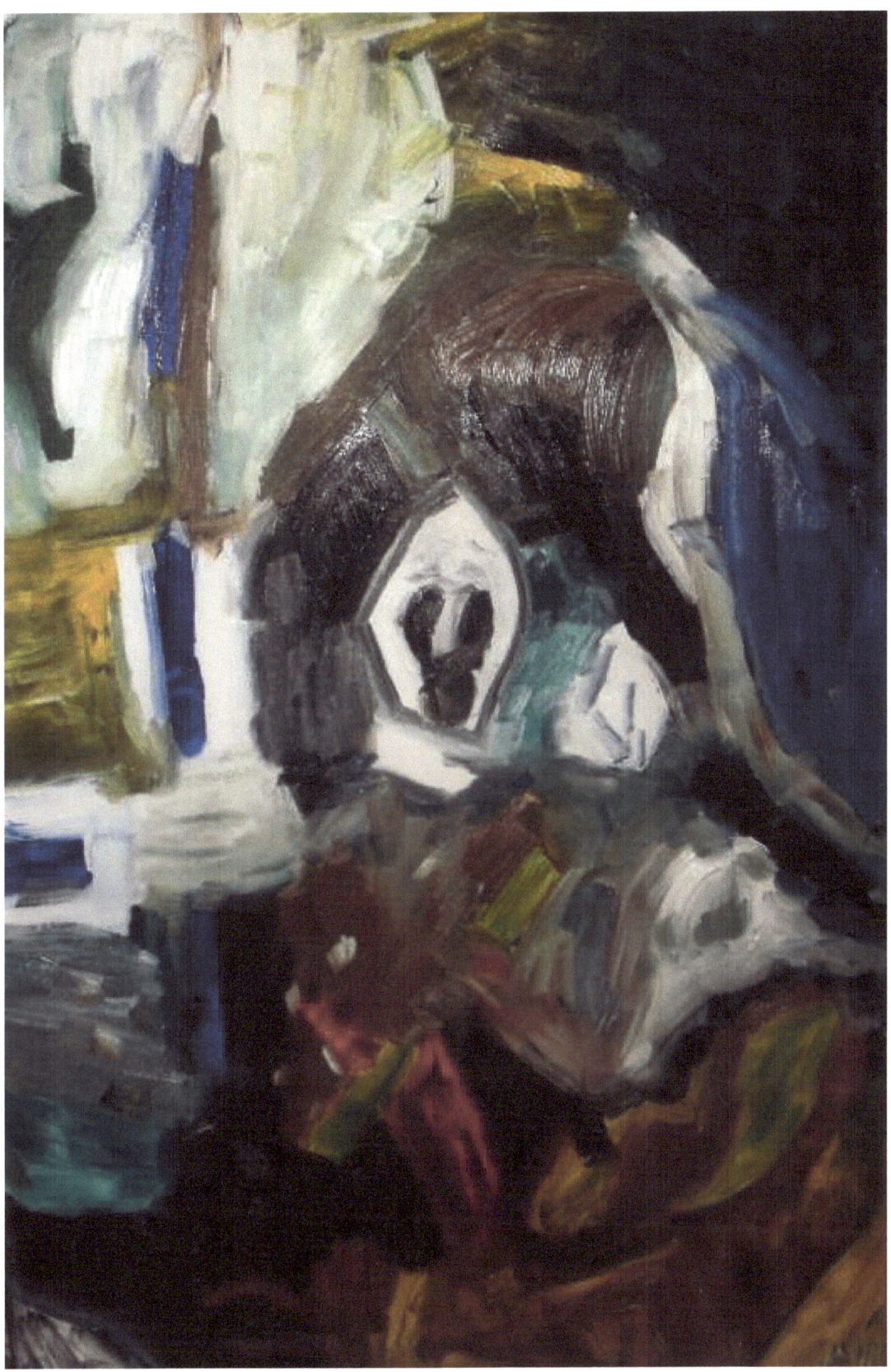

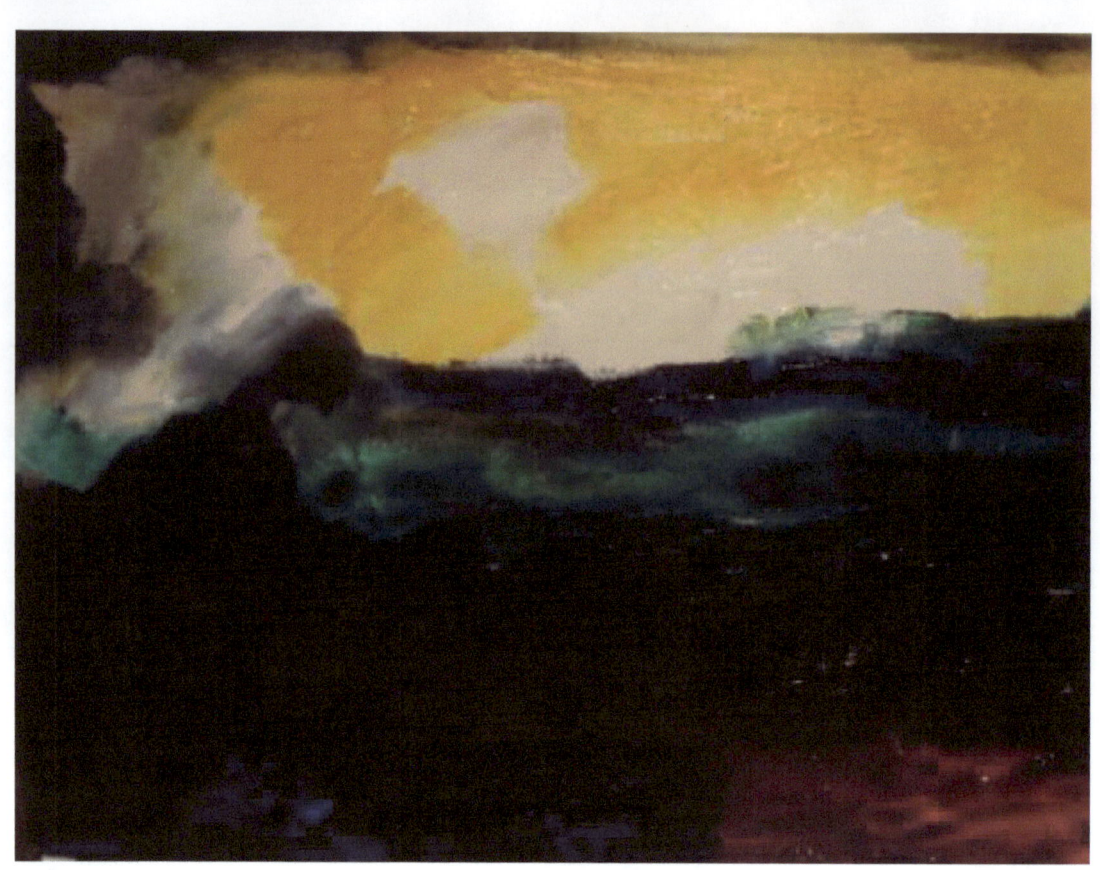

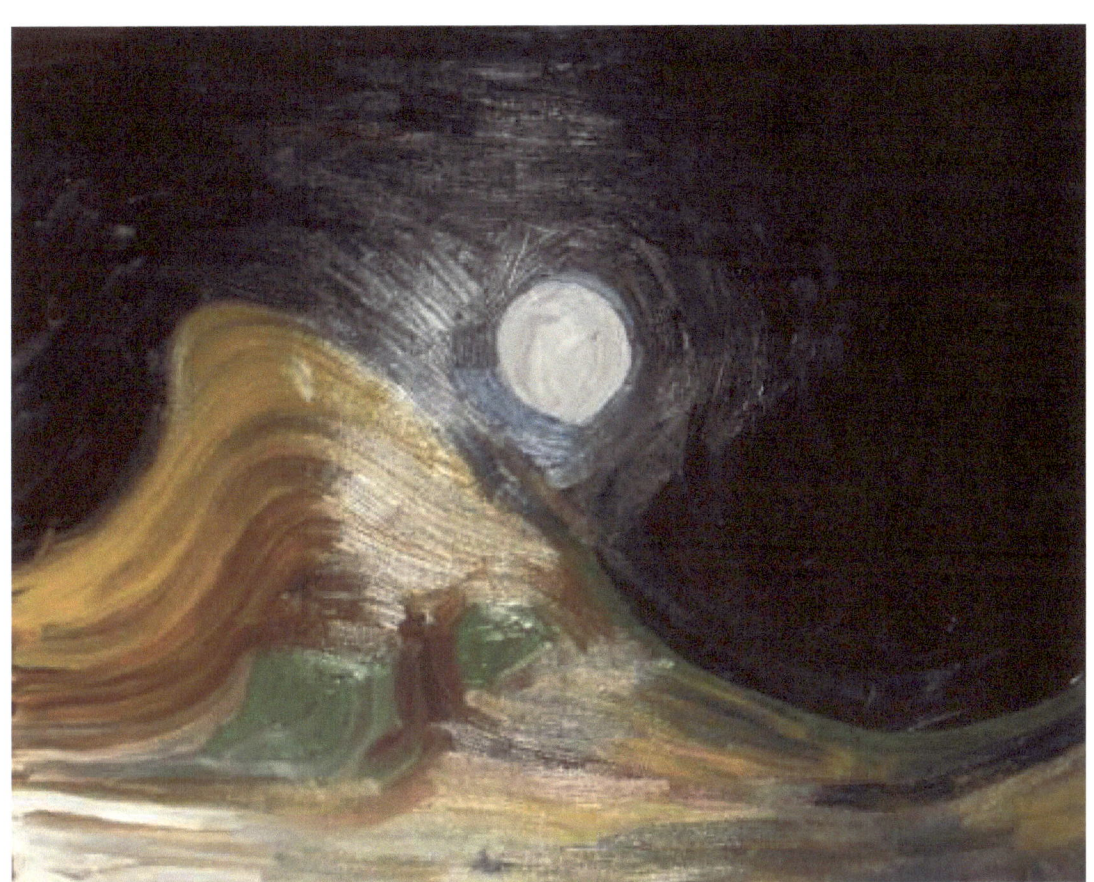

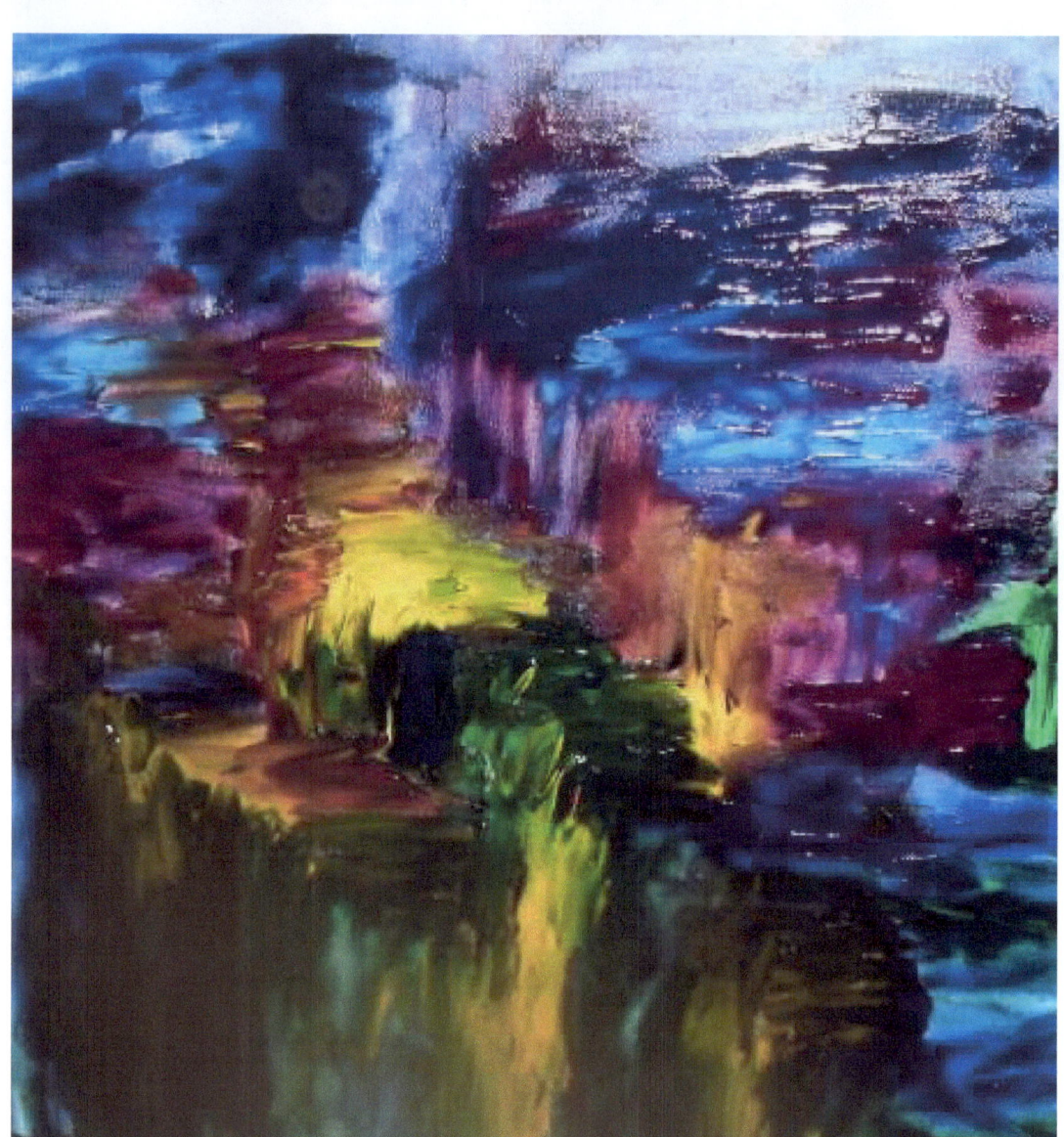

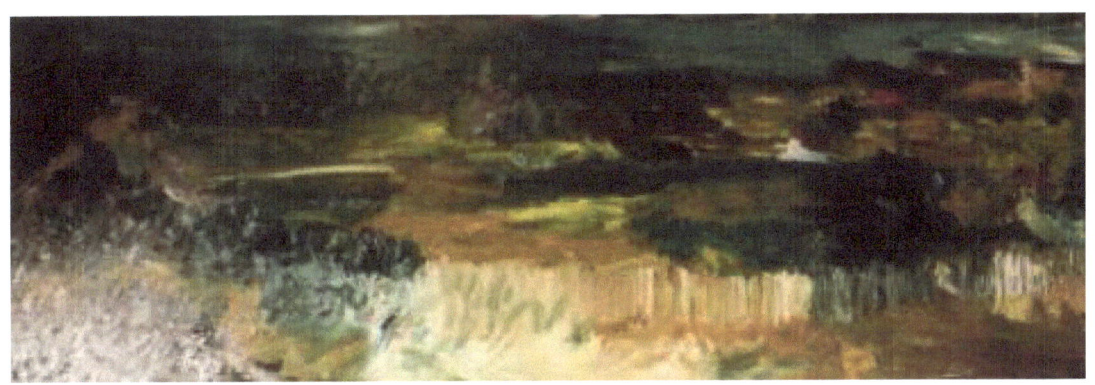

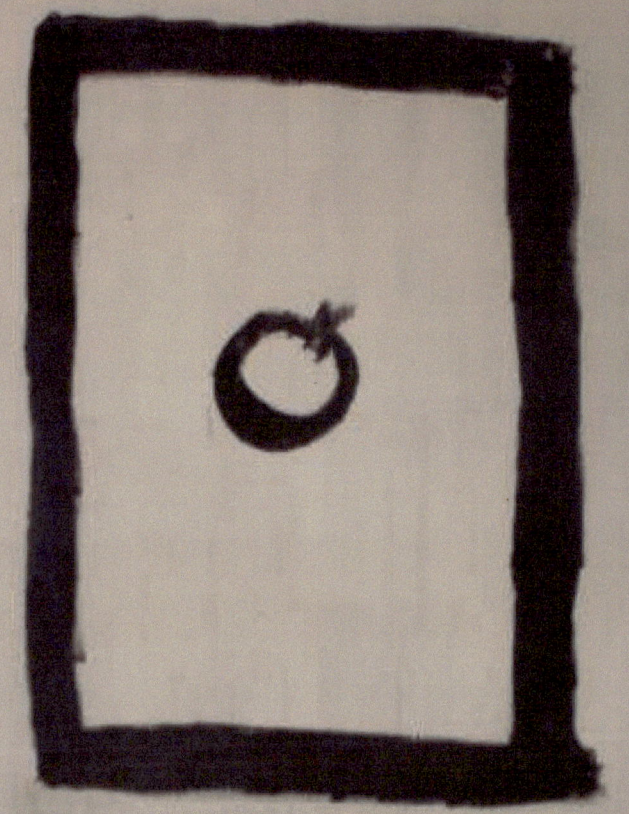

EVIL ELECTRIC AG

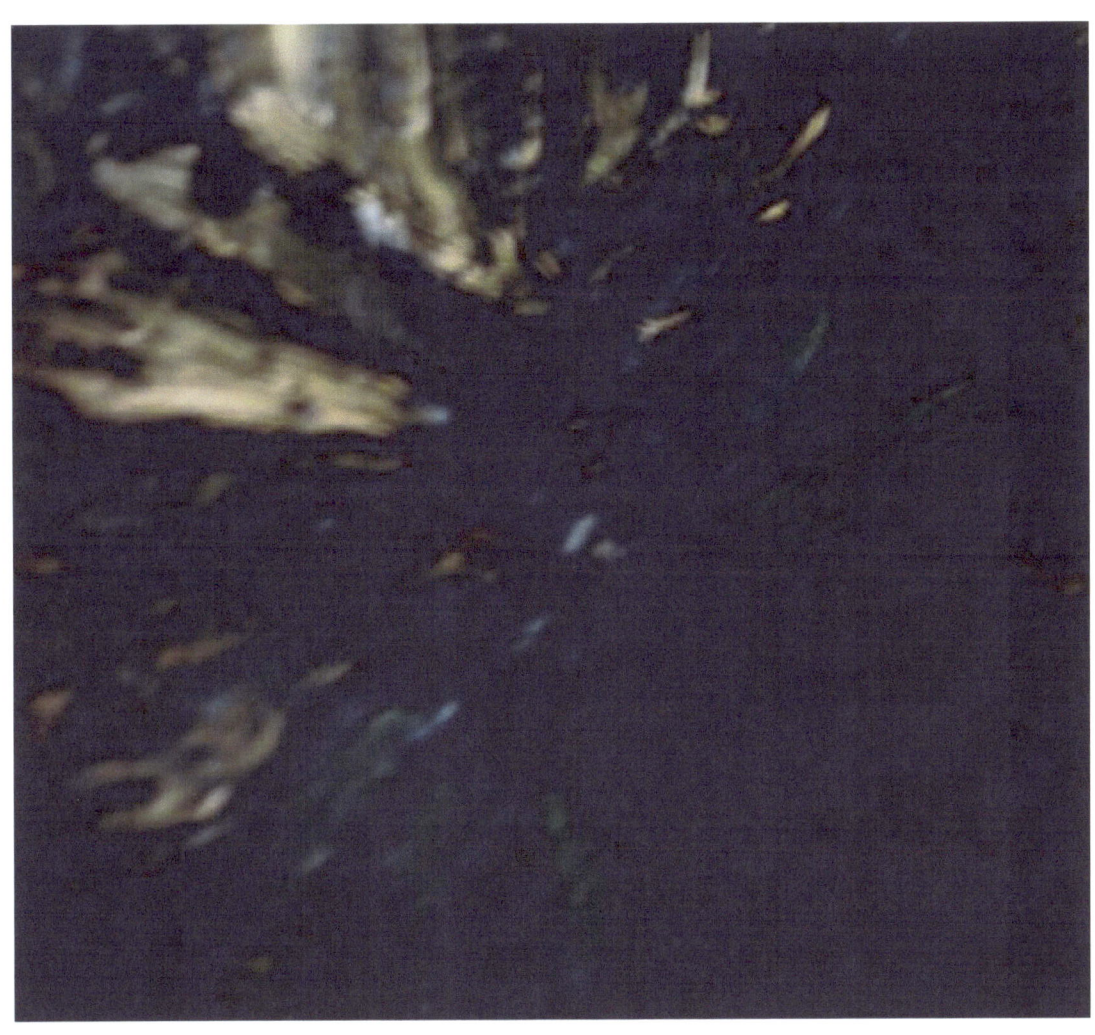

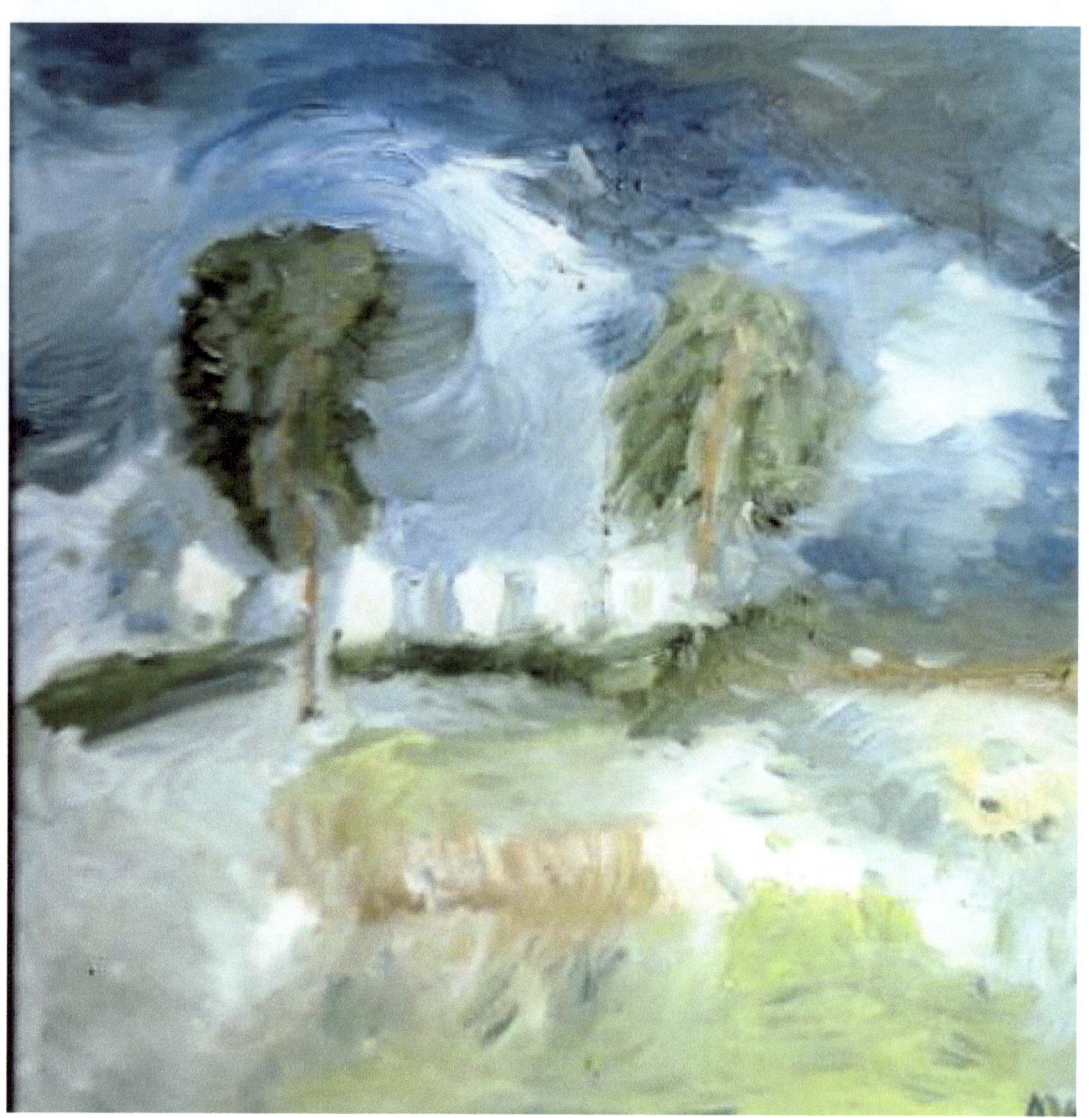

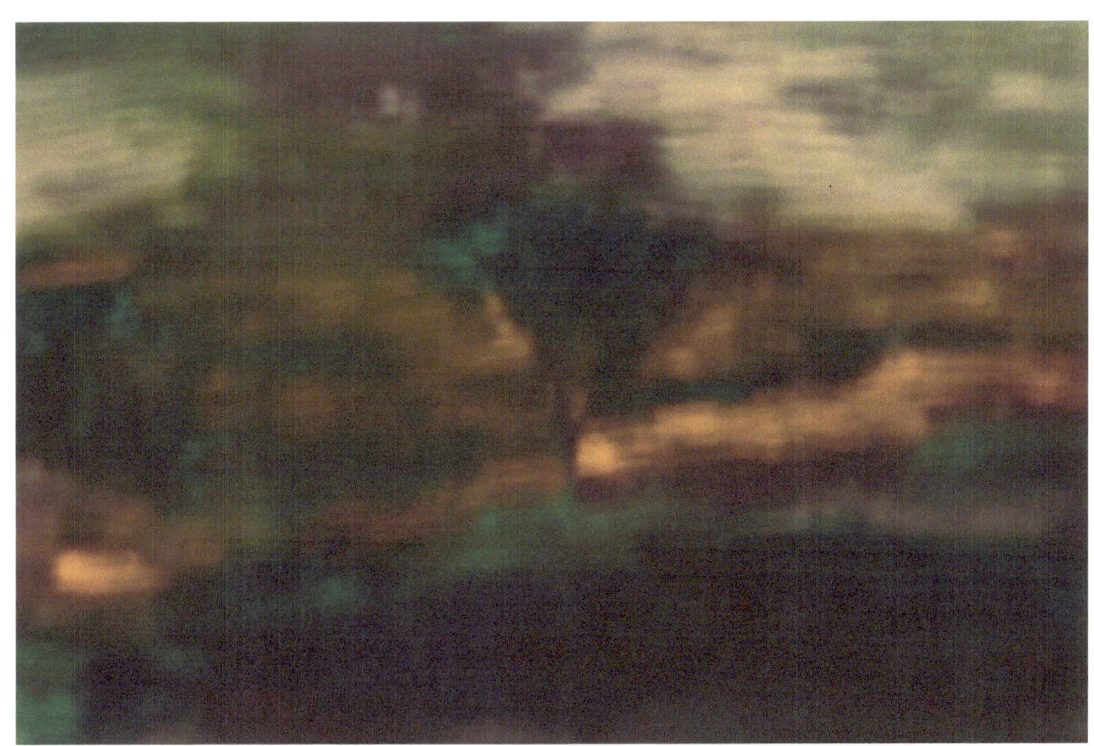

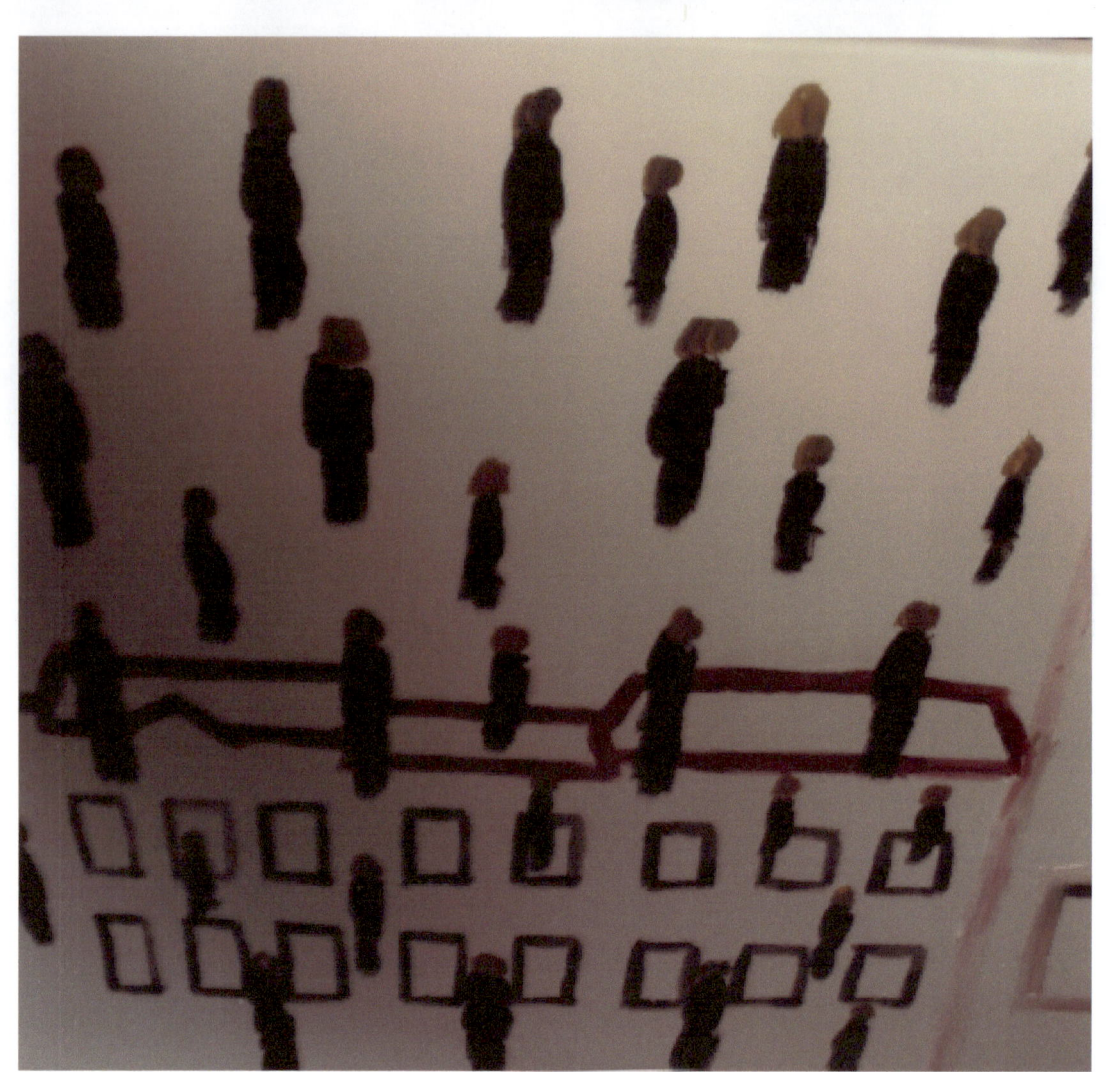

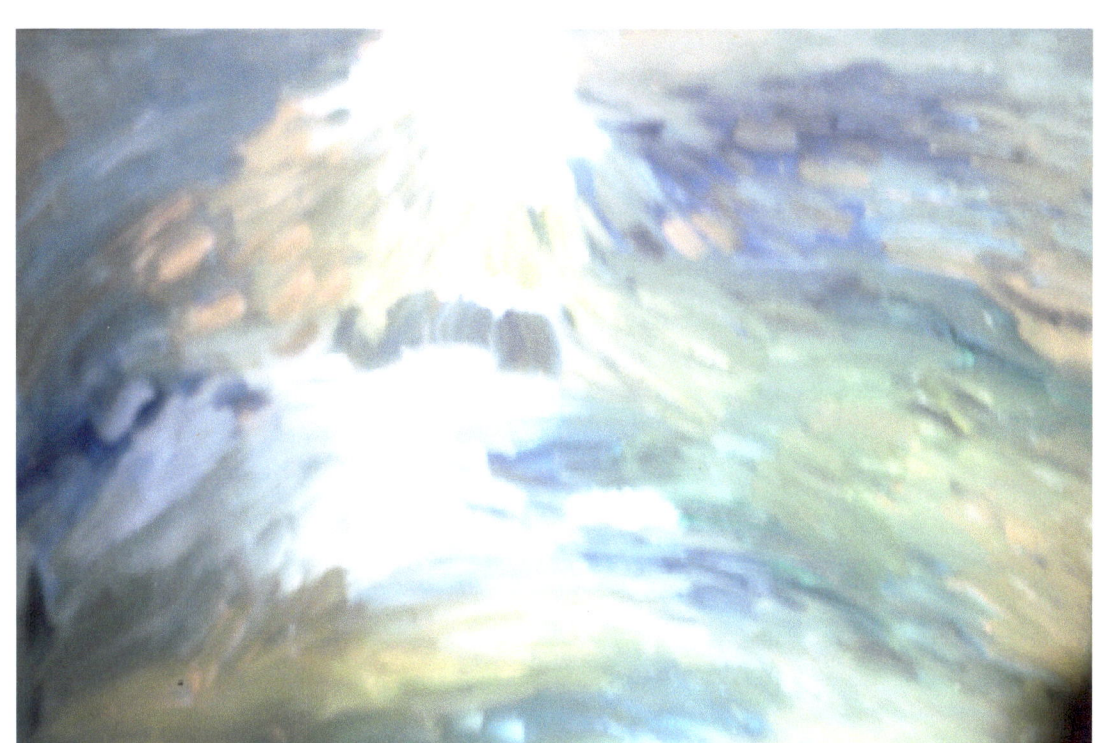

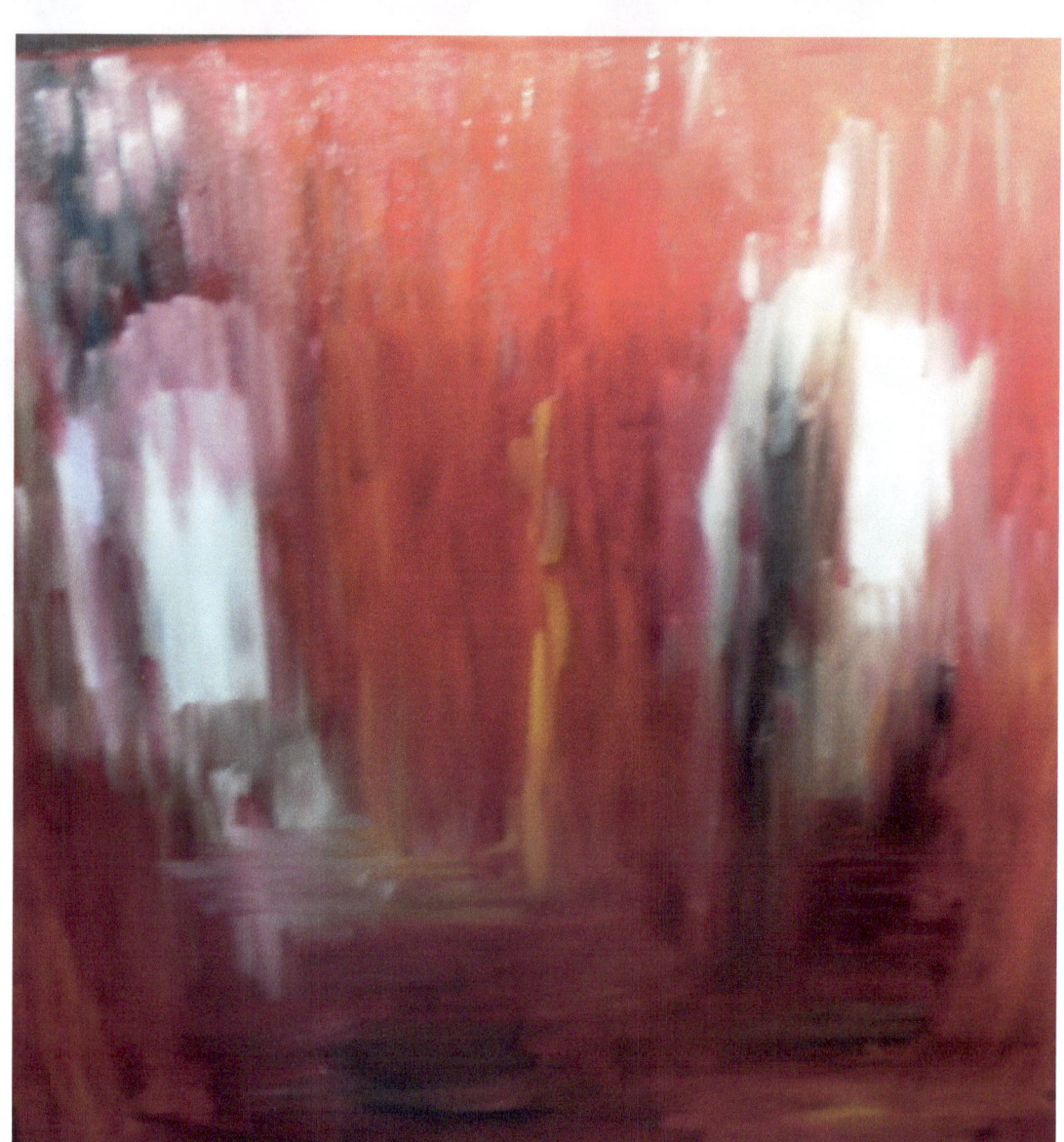

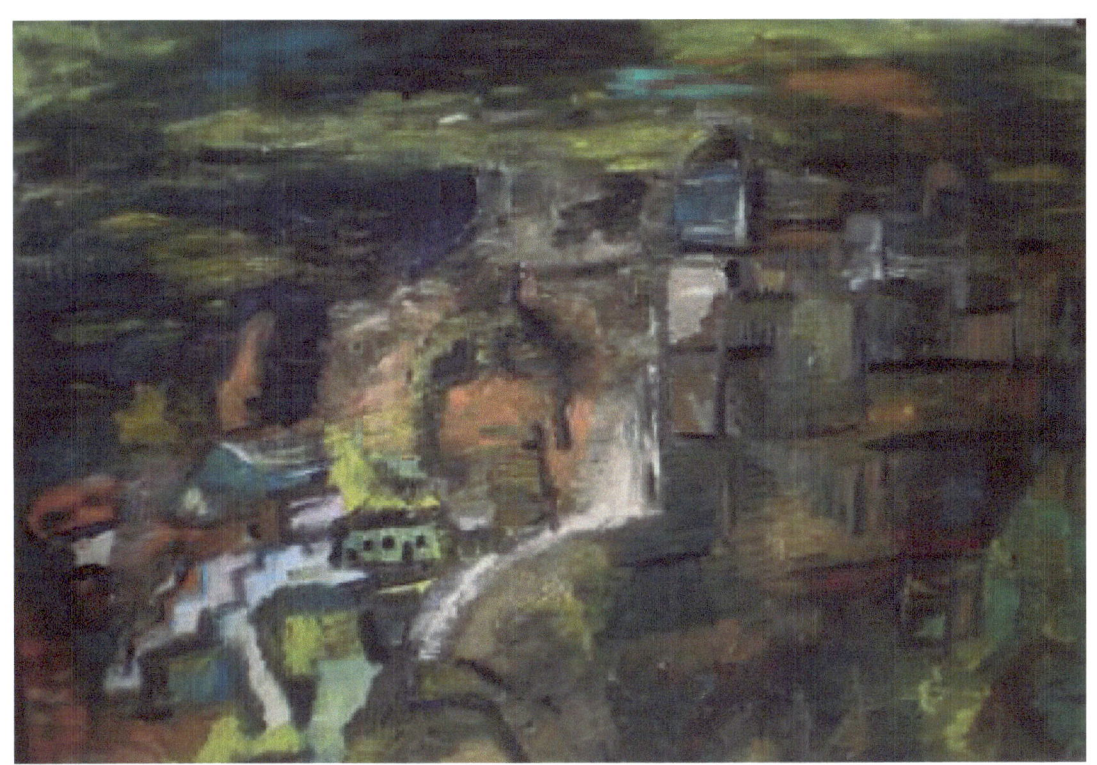

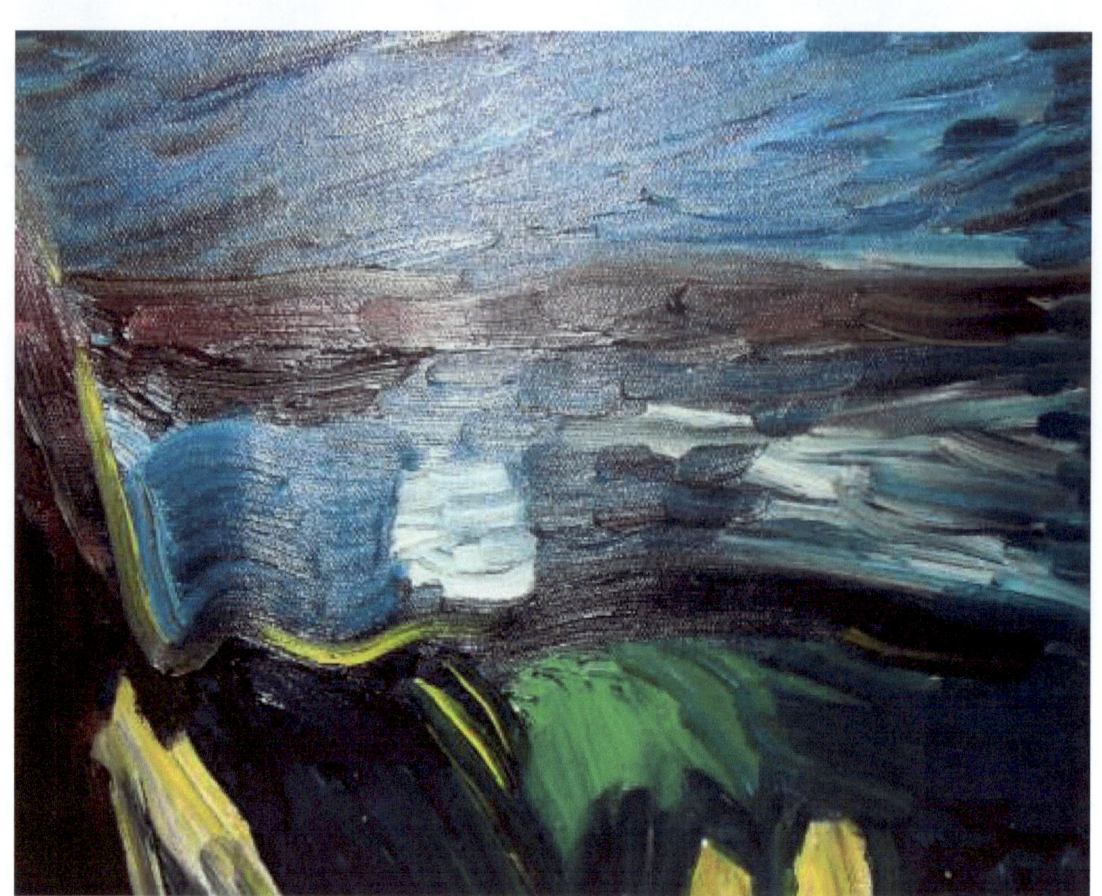

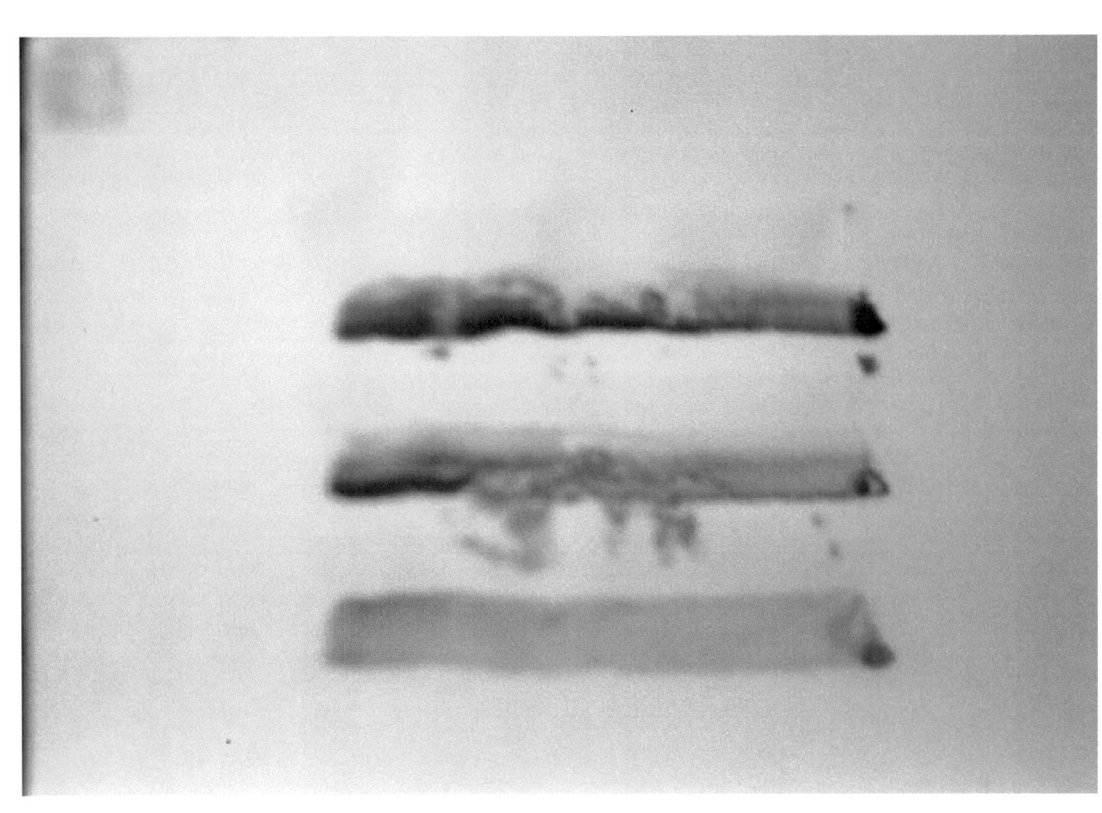

At the end of The End of the World

I saw a space ark.

www.ingramcontent.com/pod-product-compliance
Lightning Source LLC
Chambersburg PA
CBHW040745200526
45159CB00023B/1734